WILDSCHUT-EWERS: CROW BEADWORK

HE-WHO-JUMPS-OVER-EVERYONE. A CROW WARRIOR ON HORSEBACK, 1832

AFTER A WATERCOLOR BY GEORGE CATLIN

CROW INDIAN BEADWORK

A DESCRIPTIVE AND HISTORICAL STUDY

BY

WILLIAM WILDSCHUT

JOHN C. EWERS

EAGLE'S VIEW PUBLISHING

1985

Eagle's View Publishing Company
6756 North Fork Road
Liberty, Utah 84310

Library of Congress Catalog Number: 84-73388
ISBN 0-943604-06-0 in paperback
ISBN 0-943604-07-9 in hardback

Library of Congress Cataloging in Publication Data

Wildschut, William.
    Crow Indian beadrowk.

    Reprint. Originally published: New York: Museum of the Ameri-
can Indian, Heye Foundation, 1959. (Contributions from the
Museum of the American Indian, Heye Foundation; vol. 16)
    Bibliography: p.
    1. Crow Indians—Costume and adornment. 2. Crow Indians—
Industries. 3. Beadwork—Great Plains. 4. Indians of North Amer-
ica—Great Plains—Costume and adornment. 5. Indians of North
America—Great Plains—Industries. I. Ewers, John Canfield. II.
Title.
E99.C92W5   1985   746.5'08997   84-73388

CONTENTS

	PAGE
Foreword	v
Introduction	1
Men's Dress Clothing	4
Shirts	6
Leggings	8
Feather Bonnets	10
Vests	11
Gauntlets	12
Feather Fans ..	12
Women's Dress Clothing	14
Dresses	14
Leggings	16
Belts	17
Robes and Blankets	19
Moccasins	21
Riding Gear	24
Saddles	24
Head Ornaments	26
Horse Collars .	26
Cruppers	27
Saddle Blankets	28
Containers	30
Saddle Bags ...	30
Quivers	31
Gun Cases	32
Sword and Lance Cases	32
Cradles	33
Belt Pouches ..	35

PAGE

Ration Ticket Pouches 36

Mirror Pouches 36

Pipe and Tobacco Pouches 37

Characteristics of Crow Indian Beadwork 39

Beadwork Techniques 39

Beadwork Designs 41

Bead Colors 45

Symbolism in Crow Beadwork 47

History of Crow Indian Beadwork 48

Bibliography 53

ILLUSTRATIONS

PLATE   I   FRONTISPIECE

PLATE   II   FACING PAGE 26

PLATE III   FACING PAGE 34

FIGURES FOLLOW BIBLIOGRAPHY

FOREWORD

Thirty-seven years ago the late Robert H. Lowie, foremost student of the culture of the Crow Indians of Montana, published the first monograph on Crow Indian beadwork. Between the years 1907 and 1916 Dr. Lowie had made repeated visits to the Crow Reservation to study their traditional customs. Yet he has stated clearly that in his fieldwork of that period his "attention was directed almost wholly to the social and religious aspects of Crow culture." (Lowie, 1922 A, p. 203).

In 1920, when it became apparent that there was little liklihood of his resuming fieldwork among the Crow Indians, Lowie prepared two short papers on Crow material culture and arts and crafts which were based upon his incidental field notes, studies of writings of earlier travelers, and examination of museum specimens. In his introduction to the second of those papers, entitled *Crow Indian Art*, Lowie frankly wrote:

"During my frequent visits to the Crow Reservation I collected art specimens and made some observations on methods of decoration, but without ever concentrating my attention on this phase of native activity. My own collections are indeed supplemented in generous fashion by other material, mainly from the Lenders and Tefft purchases; and through Mr. G. G. Heye's courtesy I have also had access to the material in the Museum of the American Indian, Heye Foundaton. Nevertheless, I feel that my observations are inadequate even on the objective side. It is especially in approaching the delicate matter of characterizing tribal styles that the student feels the incompleteness of even a large random collection. Considering that older specimens are often of doubtful provenience, that others though certainly bought in a given locality have probably been imported from elsewhere, quite satisfactory results could be secured only from very large series of specimens from all of the tribes embraced in a survey. Since this condition was not fulfilled in the present case, my comparative results must be regarded as purely tentative and are put forth in order to be tested in the light of fuller information." (Lowie, 1922 B, p. 275).

One of the most interested readers of Lowie's paper on Crow art was William Wildschut, a business man of Billings, Montana, a town located less than 10 miles north of the Crow Reservation and frequently visited by Crow Indians. Mr. Wildschut had many friends among the Crow. He was intensely interested in their traditional culture and, in 1918, began to collect ethnological specimens among them. The year before the publication of Lowie's *Crow Indian Art* Wildschut began to collect Crow materials for the Museum of the American Indian, Heye Foundation. But Wildschut's fieldwork among the Crow went beyond the mere collection of specimens. He observed the great variety of traditional articles owned and used by the Crow Indians, and he carefully questioned the Indians regarding the tribal origin of each kind of artifact. His field studies led Wildschut to question the Crow origin of the great majority of the bead-decorated specimens described and illustrated in Lowie's *Crow Indian Art* as well as Lowie's general conclusion that "the beadwork of the Crow, especially in its most highly developed representatives, is a somewhat attenuated reflex of Dakota art." (Lowie, 1922B, p. 321).

Mr. Wildschut devoted a portion of a manuscript on the Crow Indians, which he prepared for this museum in 1927, to an explanation of the contrast between Crow Indian beadwork as described by Lowie and the beadwork of that tribe as he had come to know it. He concluded that true Crow beadwork was not borrowed from the neighboring Western Sioux, nor from any other tribe. It possessed a distinctive character of its own.

William Wildschut died in 1955. Two years later I asked John C. Ewers, formerly Associate Curator of Ethnology at the U.S. National Museum, to read Wildschut's Crow manuscript. Over a period of a quarter of a century Mr. Ewers had studied the Plains Indian collections of the larger museums in this country. He had engaged in extensive field work among the Blackfoot, Assiniboin, Western Sioux, and Flathead tribes, neighbors of the Crow Indians. Mr. Ewers was particularly impressed by the accuracy and significance of Wildschut's characterization of Crow beadwork of the first quarter of this century. He suggested that Wildschut's findings, combined with a study of Crow beadwork of earlier years, would provide a meaningful summary of what is known of this major Crow Indian craft. To further this study Ewers re-examined the early literature on this tribe, the dated pictorial materials on the Crow Indians in the Bureau of American Ethnology, the U.S.

National Museum and the National Archives in Washington, and the Crow collections in the U.S. National Museum as well as in this museum.

This publication combines the findings of William Wildschut and those of John C. Ewers. In so doing it provides both an illustrated description and a history of Crow Indian beadwork from the time of its first mention by the fur trader, François Larocque, in 1805, to the conclusion of Wildschut's field studies in 1927.

March 1959   E. K. BURNETT
                                                         Director.

FOREWORD TO THE EAGLE'S VIEW EDITION

This study remains important for a number of reasons. First, of all the Tribes of the Upper Missouri, the beadwork of the Crow Nation is most outstanding in pattern, color and craftsmanship. The beauty and use of distinctive colors has been commented on by "outsiders" as diverse as Larocque and Bodmer, and even today a visitor to the annual Crow Fair cannot help but be impressed by the beadwork in evidence.

Further, any one interested in the early explorers and fur traders find that the Crow are extremely important to this era. For reasons far too complex to delve into in this Foreword, this Nation was among the first to form alliances with the white man, a relationship that lasted through the Plains Indian Wars of the late 19th century. The popularity of this book attests to the ongoing interest in the People of Absoroka and their craftwork.

This edition was only possible with the assistance and encouragement of the Museum of the American Indian Heye Foundation and particularly with the help of Ellen Jameson and their photographic department. We owe them a great deal for their cooperation and support.

As the authors refer repeatedly to the Plates and Figures we felt it important that they be of the best quality possible. The Heye Foundation was able to find all of the color and a majority of the black and white negatives but a number of pictures had to be taken directly from the original 1959 edition. We owe the quality of this difficult process to Artistic Printing Company of Salt Lake City, Utah.

The graphics throughout this edition and the line work in Figure 41 were done by Ralph L. Smith. The classic rifle scabbard on the front cover is the work of Gary Johnson, a contemporary Crow craftsman who is second to none in the creation of Crow quill and beadwork. The cover photo was taken by Photo Productions—Kert Kley. To all of these artists we are grateful.

This edition is dedicated to John C. Ewers whose studies of the Indians of the Upper Missouri serves as examples that scholarship and sensitivity are not mutually exclusive concerns.

Monte Smith
Editor

April 1985

INTRODUCTION

THE Crow or Apsaruke Indians separated from the semi-sedentary, horticultural Hidatsa Indians on the Missouri River at least 175 years ago. When they were first described by François Larocque, a trader from Canada who traveled with them during the summer of 1805, the Crow had become a nomadic, hunting people who lived in skin-covered tipis in the valley of the Yellowstone River and its tributaries in the southeastern portion of the present state of Montana and adjacent areas in present Wyoming.

In the days before the extermination of the buffalo the Crow Indians were the Plains Indians par excellence. They were the wealthiest and the best dressed Indians in the entire Upper Missouri region. They were renowned both for their steadfast friendship toward the whites and for their courageous struggle to preserve their fine hunting grounds and large horse herds from the hostile incursions of the aggressive and more numerous Blackfoot tribes from the north and the powerful Teton Dakota (Western Sioux) from the east. After the termination of intertribal warfare and the extermination of the buffalo the Crow Indians were settled upon a large reservation, well within the area of their former hunting grounds, in southeastern Montana. Here they have been making a living as stockmen and farmers.

The prowess of the Crow Indians as warriors has received due recognition from historians and ethnologists. However, their ingenuity and skill as artists and craftsmen has not been acknowledged adequately by modern students. Especially in their evaluations of Crow Indian beadwork, the dominant Crow decorative art of the past century, have some students of the highest reputation been inclined to deprecate the originality of the Crow. In a comparative study of Plains Indian beadwork, published 50 years ago, A. L. Kroeber wrote: "The Crow appear to be intermediate between the Blackfeet and Sioux." (Kroeber, 1908, p. 156). Less than 25 years ago Robert H. Lowie claimed that "Crow women seem to have evolved an embroidery style under Dakota and Blackfoot influences." (Lowie, 1935, p. 81).

Why Crow Indian women would have been busy copying the beadwork of the enemy Blackfoot and Dakota tribes while their

1   I

husbands were risking their lives to preserve their tribe from
domination by the same enemies has not been explained. Nor can
it be explained. The unusual richness of the Crow country in the
natural resources needed for craft work, the repeated references to
the excellence of Crow crafts in the nineteenth century, the testi-
mony of Crow Indians in the field in the 1920s, and a careful
analysis of well-documented museum specimens all testify to the
quality, variety and originality of Crow crafts and their relative
independence of influences from neighboring tribes.

Certainly one of the factors which enabled Crow women to excell
as craftworkers was the richness of the historic tribal habitat in
basic materials employed in craftwork. A century ago the knowl-
edgeable fur trader, Edwin T. Denig, described the Crow country
east of the Bighorn Mountains as "perhaps the best game country
in the world." (Denig, 1953, p. 21). Immense herds of buffalo
grazed on the grasslands extending from the mountains eastward
to the mouth of the Yellowstone. Elk and deer (both black and
white-tailed) were numerous in the river bottoms. Antelopes
were plentiful on the plains. Bighorn sheep and grizzly bears
abounded in the nearby mountains. These animals, together with
the common porcupine, furnished most of the materials needed
by the Plains Indian craftworker. In the territory of no other
tribe of the Upper Missouri were they found in such variety and
abundance.

We know that the earliest descriptions of the Crow Indians
tell of their trading buffalo skin lodges, buffalo robes, skin shirts,
leggings, and other articles of apparrel to the horticultural Mandan
and Hidatsa on the Missouri. (Ewers, 1954, pp. 433–434, 438–439).
This is indicative of the industry of Crow women in such crafts as
skin dressing, and the making of clothing in sufficient quantities to
provide items for export as well as for their tribal needs.

We know, also, that the Crow Indians were among the first of
the Upper Missouri groups to employ trade beads in their decorative arts. When Larocque met the Crow in 1805 he saw that they
already possessed "small blue glass beads that they get from the
Spaniards but by the second and third man" through Shoshoni
intermediaries who traded with the Spaniards of the Southwest.
So fond of these beads were the Crow that they gave a horse for
100 of them. Larocque observed that the Crow decorated their
clothing with beads as well as with porcupine quills Larocque
himself repeatedly exchanged blue beads for beaver pelts with

Crow hunters. (Larocque, 1910, pp. 22–36, 42, 45, 68). The Crow preference for blue beads persisted into the present century.

Unlike the Blackfoot and the Sioux, whose great fondness for liquor caused them to prefer it to most other goods offered by white traders, the Crow Indians in the first half of the nineteenth century were teetotalers. Charles Larpenteur, who traded with the Crow in 1833, noted the effect of their abstinence upon the appearance of these Indians:

"As they do not drink, their trade was all in substantial goods, which kept them well dressed, and extremely rich in horses; so it was really a beautiful sight to see that tribe on the move." (Larpenteur, 1898, Vol. I. p. 45).

Two decades later Denig referred to the wealth of the Crow, their discretion in selecting the finest goods of European manufacture which the traders had to offer, and the elegance of Crow costume. He observed that a Crow camp on the march "presents a gay and lively appearance, more so perhaps than any other [tribe]." (Denig, 1953, pp. 25, 33, 35, 71).

It was in the decoration of those articles that could be seen when camp was on the march to visit the Mandan and Hidatsa on the Missouri or one of the trading posts of the whites that Crow Indian women lavished their care and skill as beadworkers. These objects were of three major types—the dress clothing worn by the Indians, the riding gear placed on their horses, and the containers employed in holding and transporting a variety of articles of different sizes, shapes and functions.

Let us consider each class of these bead-ornamented articles in turn.

1*

MEN'S DRESS CLOTHING

When Larocque was among the Crow Indians in 1805 he observed that the young, single men were especially fond of fancy clothing but "the married men dress fine but when they rise the camp and on certain occasions." (Larocque, 1910, p. 61). His de scription of Crow men's garb referred to the clothing worn on special occasions rather than to their everyday costume. The principal body garments were leggings of antelope skin "reaching to the hips, the end tucked in a belt or girdle the seam ornamented with beads, porcupine quills and human hair dyed with divers Colours," and shirts of the same materials "composed of 3 skins, 2 making the body and one the Sleeves, the skins are joint together in the shoulder only & the sleeves also which are left open under the pit of the arm; the neck of one of the skins hangs on the breast and the other behind and are garnished on the sleeves with the same materials as the Leggins." Men seldom wore breech clouts "except when they do not put on leggins, as their leggins are so made that if they had a waist band they might be called trousers." (Larocque, 1910, pp. 66–67).[1]

By the time George Catlin and Prince Maximilian visited the tribes of the Upper Missouri a quarter century later (1832 and 1833 respectively), the breech clout was commonly worn by men of all of the tribes of that region. Both Catlin and Maximilian had ample opportunity to compare the clothing of the Upper Missouri tribes, and they independently came to the same conclusion regarding the superiority of the garments made by the Crow Indians.

Catlin wrote that the Crow "may be justly said to be the most beautifully clad of all the Indians in these regions." (Catlin, 1841, Vol. I. p. 191). Our frontispiece reproduces Catlin's portrait of He-Who-Jumps-Over-Everyone, a Crow warrior on horseback, wearing a shirt and leggings of "mountain-goat skins, beautifully

[1] The inference is that Crow men's leggings at that time were so made as to cover the privates, perhaps with crossed flaps, so that no breech clout was necessary. Fifty years ago Edward Curtis reported a Crow tradition to the effect that: "In the old time they had no loincloth; indeed as late as seventy-five years ago some of the old men had not yet adopted that article of dress." (Curtis, 1909, Vol. 4. p. 23).

4

dressed and their seams everywhere fringed with a profusion of scalp locks taken from the heads of his enemies slain in battle." (*Idem*, p. 191).[2]

Maximilian considered that the Crow and Hidatsa surpassed all other tribes of the Upper Missouri in the elegance of their clothing. At the same time he noted that the shirts worn by Hidatsa men were obtained by barter from the Crow, and stated that "Crow women are very skillfull in various kinds of work, and their shirts and dresses of bighorn leather, embroidered and ornamented with dyed porcupine quills, are particularly handsome." (Maximilian, Vol. 22. pp. 352–353; 359–360).

Carl Bodmer, the talented young artist who accompanied Prince Maximilian, portrayed a Crow Indian clothed in a long skin shirt and tight fitting skin leggings. The shirt was decorated with a large quilled rosette over the wearer's chest and panels of quill-work covering the long sleeve seams in which cross designs (possibly in beadwork) appear prominently. Both shirt and leggings also were decorated with painted stripes. (See Fig. 1, man at far left).

Beadwork must have been of secondary importance to porcupine quillwork in the decoration of Crow men's clothing at that time, for neither Catlin nor Maximilian mentioned the use of beads on men's shirts or leggings, nor did either Catlin or Bodmer picture men's garments showing any prominent use of beads in their decoration. Nevertheless, Father De Smet, writing of his reception by the Crow Indians in the summer of 1842, stated: "All the chiefs and warriors were habited in their embroidered moccasins, leggings and buckskin shirts ornamented with beads and porcupine quills." (Chittenden and Richardson, Vol. 3, p. 1036).

When General Raynolds met the Crow during his exploration of the Yellowstone River Valley in 1857, he noted that the full dress of the chiefs and prominent warriors included not only "moccasins ornamented with beads" but also "leggings of skin, embroided with beads and porcupine quills dyed the most brilliant colors, and a large outer covering somewhat resembling the Mexican serape, but made of skin richly decorated." (Raynolds, 1868, p. 48). He observed that the common (everyday) dress of the Crow at that time was not of skins but "woolen clothing, such as pantaloons, shirts, and hats."

[2] Catlin may well have mistaken the mountain goat skin for that of the mountain sheep (bighorn) which was favored for dress clothing.

Although some of the members of the Crow Indian delegation to Washington in 1873 wore quilled shirts, all of the prominent Crow leaders in the delegation of 1880 wore beaded shirts, leggings and moccasins. (See the photograph of this delegation reproduced as Fig. 2).

SHIRTS

The oldest and most unusual Crow beaded shirt in the collections of the Museum of the American Indian is a war shirt, which belonged originally to Buffalo Bull, collected by Wildschut in 1922 (CAT. 12/3099). See Fig. 3.

This short garment of heavy skin (probably buffalo-hide) has no neck flap and no true sleeves. The short (13") extensions over the upper arms hang loose underneath. The beaded decoration is limited to narrow bands over each shoulder composed of lavender seed beads divided into blocky segments by narrow, transverse stripes of dark blue and of red beads; and to broader bands in the same colors extending inward to the neck opening which are flanked by pairs of small isosceles triangles (of green, red, yellow and blue beads) with their apices touching the bands. The surface of the shirt is covered with black paint.

Even though this shirt may be of an earlier type, it is doubtful if the specimen was decorated prior to 1870, for all the beads are of the smaller seed bead kind rather than of the larger pony beads commonly employed on the older specimens of beadwork of the tribes of the Northern Plains region.

More typical of the form and decoration of the Crow man's dress shirt worn in the last three decades of the 19th century is the one illustrated in Fig. 4. (CAT. 3/2909 MAIHF). The skin background of this shirt is painted a blue green. Hair pendants hang from the borders of the neck flaps and the beaded arm panels, and strips of white (winter) weasel skins are pendant from the shoulder panels. The neck flaps (identical at front and back) are rectangular pieces of skin (each $8\frac{3}{4}'' \times 4''$) and each is decorated with a narrow border and three horizontal bands of beadwork applied in the lazy stitch. The beaded arm panels are $2\frac{1}{4}''$ wide. They consist of central areas composed of five vertical bands (three of lavender and two of green beads) flanked by narrow transverse stripes of dark blue and yellow beads, and large blocks of light blue beads. The blocks of blue beads are applied in a modification of the lazy stitch commonly employed by Crow beadworkers. (See Fig. 41C). The over-shoulder panels are similar in color, design and technique to those on the arms except that they are bordered by narrow bands of white and dark blue beads applied in the lazy stitch. (See Fig. 41B).

That the beaded rectangular neck flap was used on Crow men's shirts before 1860 is clearly indicated in a portrait of a Crow chief taken by the photographer of the Raynolds Expedition and reproduced in Hayden, 1862, Fig. 1.

A shirt bearing a beaded decoration almost identical to the one just described was worn by Long Horse, a member of the Crow delegation to Washington in 1873. Another member of that group, Old Crow, wore a shirt decorated with porcupine quilled arm and shoulder panels bearing similar horizontal banded designs. This suggests that this simple composition in the decoration of arm and shoulder panels was adapted from quillwork to beadwork.[3]

The shirts worn by Crow men on dress occasions in the early years of the present century were similar in form to the one pictured in Fig. 4. They possessed rectangular, beaded neck flaps and beaded arm and shoulder panels. However, the patterned central portions of the panels were usually of more complex design, commonly consisting of a horizontal central band flanked by triangles, or of a large hourglass form.

The section of a shirt illustrated in Fig. 5 provides a relatively simple example of the type. (CAT. 22/1697 MAIHF). The central bands are flanked by angular areas in lavender beads and dark blue, broad-based triangles. The large blocks of solid color are in light blue beads. Notice that both arm and shoulder panels have narrow borders, that the band of beadwork flanked by triangles in the area between shoulder band and neck opening resembles similar treatment of this area on the shirt portrayed in Fig. 3. On this shirt the triangles in the shoulder bands are outlined with a narrow border of white beads applied in the overlaid stitch. (See Fig. 41A.) Otherwise the beadwork techniques are the same as those employed in the decoration of the shirt shown in Fig. 4.

Examination of a number of Crow men's shirts collected in the late years of the 19th century and in the early years of the present one reveals that Crow beadworkers had a marked preference for the use of light blue beads as backgrounds for the arm and shoulder

---

[3] Reference is made to Bureau of American Ethnology negatives 3,382 and 3,381.

panel design areas. Occasionally they substituted lavender beads for those of light blue.

LEGGINGS

A clue to the probable use of beads in combination with porcupine quills in the decoration of men's shirts and leggings, mentioned by white men who observed the Crow Indians prior to 1850, appears in the specimen illustrated in Fig. 6. (CAT. 1/6931 MAIHF). The legging decoration consists primarily of a panel of five vertical bands of porcupine quillwork and the major motifs are large, outlined rectangles.[4] Beads were used in narrow borders flanking the quilled panel and in two transverse bands on the red flannel cuff. All of the beads are of the larger pony bead type commonly appearing on the older specimens of bead embroidery from the Upper Missouri tribes. These beads were expensive and usually were used rather sparingly by Indian craftswomen.

A pencil sketch of two Crow Indian visitors to Fort Union at the mouth of the Yellowstone, drawn by the Swiss artist, Rudolph Kurz, on November 29, 1851, appears to show a beaded legging worn by the man on the left. See Fig. 7. The design is composed of hourglass shapes formed of two tall isosceles triangles with apices joined. These are elaborated with smaller isosceles triangles touching their bases.

Fig. 8 illustrates one of a pair of beaded skin leggings collected among the Crow Indians by the artist, Edwin W. Deming, who visited the tribe in the early 1890s. (CAT. 1/1067 MAIHF). The beaded panel, 27" long by $3\frac{1}{4}$" wide, provides an excellent example of Crow use of symmetry in beadwork design. The panel is divided into five sections, of which the two end ones and the center section are relatively plain, composed of broad central rectangles in light blue beads, flanked by narrower rectangles in lavender beads. The second and fourth sections are more elaborate, yet they are identical except that the right-angled triangles in the two sections point in opposite directions (*i.e.* each toward the center of the panel). The triangles in both sections are paired (red, dark blue and red) against a light blue background and the pairs are separated by a central band in contrasting colored beads. The entire

---

[4] Note that a similar rectangle appears on the beaded leggings worn by the man on the far right in the picture of the Crow delegation of 1880. Fig. 2.

PLATE 2

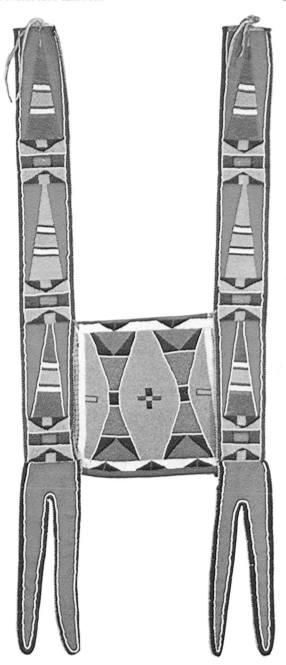

CROW BEADED HORSE COLLAR
MAIHF CAT. NO. 20/7717. LENGTH, 42 IN.

panel is symmetrical both laterally and vertically. Two bands of
seed beads border the flannel cuff much as do the pony beads on
the quilled and beaded legging shown in Fig. 6.

Women who made entire men's suits of animal skins usually
employed the same beaded designs on the legging panels as they
used on the arm and shoulder panels of the shirts so that the three
pieces of a man's suit would have matching beaded decoration.
However, by Wildschut's time (*ca.* 1920) very few buckskin leggings were to be found among the Crow Indians. For years they
had preferred loose-fitting leggings of trade cloth to their traditional tight-fitting ones of antelope, bighorn or buckskin.

Crow men began to wear leggings of blanket material, made to
match hooded coats of striped trade blanket cloth prior to the
middle of the 19th century. Kurz described a young Crow warrior
who visited Fort Union in January, 1852, wearing "Coat, leggings
and hood fashioned from a new Mackinaw blanket." (Kurz, 1937,
p. 259). The artist, Charles Wimar drew a pencil sketch of a Crow
man clad in striped cloth leggings whom he saw on his travels up
the Missouri in 1858. The stripes in the blanketing were used to
provide decoration for the lower portion of these loosefitting cloth
leggings. See Fig. 9.

Later the Crow Indians came to prefer blanket materials for
dress leggings and the women decorated these cloth leggings in
broad panels on the lower portions of the garments only. As early
as 1873 the majority of the Crow delegates to Washington wore
cloth leggings with their skin shirts. The three men in the center
of the front row in the picture of the 1880 delegation (Fig. 2) certainly wore cloth leggings. The general pattern of the beadwork on
the leggings worn by Chief Plenty Coups (second from the right in
that photograph), is one that appears in many later photographs
of Crow men in dress costumes as well as in museum collections of
Crow Indian clothing.

A good example of this type of legging, one of a pair collected
by Wildschut in 1923, is shown in Fig. 10. (CAT. 11/7687 MAIHF).
This legging is of black-striped, blue blanket cloth. Buckskin tie
strings were used to confine the lower portion of the legging to the
wearer's leg, allowing the back portion to flare at the sides much
like cowboys' chaps. However, the Wimar sketch (Fig. 9) is proof
that Crow Indians were wearing these flaring garments some years
before cowboys first invaded the Montana plains. To the front of
the lower portion of this legging was sewn a rectangular piece of

red flannel which was decorated with a narrow border of white beads and vertical bands of white beads, elaborated with slanting dark blue stripes and small isosceles triangles. Above this panel was sewn a triangular piece of red flannel decorated with a narrow beaded border, narrow horizontal band and small beaded triangles touching each angle of the larger triangle. All the beadwork was applied in the lazy stitch.

One further change in the decoration of Crow men's leggings took place within the Reservation Period. A field photograph labeled "Crow warriors" and dated July, 1895, in the photographic files of the Bureau of American Ethnology portrays one of them wearing cloth leggings decorated with beadwork in elaborate floral designs. By the 1920s floral patterns had almost entirely replaced geometric ones in the ornamentation of the cloth leggings worn by men of this tribe.

FEATHER BONNETS

The tribal origin of the eagle feather bonnet, which within the last half century has been so widely adopted by Indian tribes in all parts of the country that it has become a picturesque symbol of Indianness, cannot be determined with any degree of certainty at this late date. However, Capt. William P. Clark, while traveling widely among the Plains Indians in the early 1880s to gather data for his study of the sign language, found that the "Crow Indians are, by some tribes, given the credit of inventing this head-dress." (Clark, 1885, p. 398). Certainly Catlin pictured feather bonnets worn by both the Crow warrior, He-Who-Jumps-Over-Everyone, and by his favorite horse in the summer of 1832. (See Frontispiece). The brow bands of both of these bonnets appear to have been decorated with porcupine quills rather than with trade beads.

Wildschut found that the beaded brow bands which commonly appeared on the feather bonnets worn by Crow men in the 1920s were usually imported from the Sioux or were beaded by Cree Indians who lived among the Crow. These brow bands, generally beaded in the lazy stitch, had backgrounds of white beads and simple designs of dark-colored triangles. Such a brow band appears in the portrait of Holds His Enemy, taken during his visit to Washington in 1910. See Fig. 11.

Plenty Coups, the most renowned Crow chief of the present century, seems to have preferred a brow band on which the designs appeared in the form of tall, stepped triangles, common elements in the beadwork of the neighboring Blackfoot tribes. When he visited Washington in 1913 he wore a feather bonnet on which the stepped triangles appear against a background of darker colored beads. See Fig. 12.

In formal ceremonies at Arlington Cemetery on Nov. 11, 1921, Chief Plenty Coups placed a magnificent feather bonnet upon the casket of the Unknown Soldier of World War I as a tribute from all the American Indians to our country's unknown dead. This bonnet, which hangs in the trophy room of the Amphitheatre at Arlington, has a brow band divided into seven sections, consisting of four blocks of light blue beads, separated by three stepped triangles in lavender beads outlined with small squares of blue beads. The technique is overlaid stitch. Although the stepped triangles may have been borrowed from Blackfoot beadwork, the selection of colors and the overall composition of the beadwork appears to be typically Crow.[5]

VESTS

The wearing of vests by Plains Indians was, of course, an adoption of a white man's garment. According to Ewers' field data the beaded vest became popular among the young men of the Oglala Sioux about the year before the Custer Battle (*i.e. ca.* 1875). Considerable numbers of elaborately beaded vests from the Upper Missouri tribes, collected in the late years of the 19th century and early years of this century are preserved in museum collections.

Although many Crow Indian men wore beaded vests on dress occasions in the early years of the present century, Wildschut found that the majority of these garments were obtained from other tribes. All of the vests beaded in the lazy stitch, bearing white backgrounds and designs like those illustrated in Figures 13, 14 and 15 of Lowie's *Crow Indian Art* were intrusive.

The vests beaded by Crow Indian women, on the other hand, bore floral designs or representations of elk, horses or mounted warriors against the pale blue background so characteristic of Crow beadwork of the Reservation Period. During World War I there was a short period when the Crow beaders could not obtain

[5] A Signal Corps photograph of this bonnet is in The National Archives, Neg. SC–74459.

blue beads. But even then they substituted colored backgrounds rather than white ones. They applied the beads in long, horizontal lines extending the entire width of half of the front of the garment, except where the floral or realistic designs intervened. And they tied these long lines of beadwork down at intervals with the modified lazy stitch technique.

A typical Crow beaded vest bearing floral designs was worn by Holds-His-Enemy during his visit to Washington in 1910. See Fig. 11. Another was worn by White Hip in the field photograph appearing in Lowie 1922A, Fig. 14.

GAUNTLETS

The wearing of gloves, like the use of vests, was a custom adopted by the Plains Indians from the whites. In the early years of the 19th century Crow Indians wore mittens of buffalo hide with the hair inside as protection for the hands from the winter cold. But the custom of wearing five-fingered gloves in the summer season and simply for their decorative effect was one learned from the whites toward the end of the 19th century.

The long, broad cuffs of leather gauntlets afforded Crow bead-workers large surfaces for ornamentation. In 1913, when Plenty Coups, Medicine Crow and White Man Runs Him were photographed in Washington, they all wore buckskin gauntlets with floral beaded cuffs. Plenty Coups is wearing a pair of them in the photograph taken at that time and here reproduced as Fig. 12.

In the 1920s floral designs predominated in the beadwork on Crow gauntlets. However, a beaded horse or elk was sometimes substituted for the floral beadwork.[6]

FEATHER FANS

A feather fan was a common accessory to costume for the well-dressed Crow Indian. Notice that the man standing at the far left in Bodmer's drawing of a group of Crow Indians executed in 1833 carries the entire wing of a large bird in his right hand. (See Fig. 1).

In more recent years Crow Indians preferred a fan composed of one or two eagle feathers with red flannel wrapped around their bases to provide a convenient hand hold. This cloth commonly

[6] White Hip wore floral-beaded gauntlets in the field photograph reproduced in Lowie, 1922A, Fig. 14.

was decorated with parallel bands of beadwork, each subdivided by transverse stripes into segments of different solid colors. A fan decorated in this way was carried by Medicine Crow on his visit to Washington in 1880. (See Fig. 2, seated man second from the left). Another was carried by Plenty Coups while he was in the capital city 33 years later. (See Fig. 12).[7]

[7] A similar decoration appears on the red flannel wrappings of eagle feather pendants attached to the Crow coup sticks which Plenty Coups placed upon the coffin of the Unknown Soldier of World War I in 1921. The three narrow bands of beadwork on each piece of red flannel were applied in the lazy stitch. The colors are predominantly light blue, with transverse stripes in dark blue, and center rectangles in yellow seed beads. The apices of three small isosceles triangles touch the sides of the lowermost bands of beadwork in each ornament. This decoration is typical of Crow workmanship in design, color and method of bead application.

WOMEN'S DRESS CLOTHING

DRESSES

François Larocque described the Crow woman's dress of the period 1805 as follows:

". . . their shift or cottilion reaches mid leg and lower and is made of Elk skin, but the fine ones are made of two large Cabri [antelope] or Mountain Ram [bighorn] skins, like the man's shirts the bottom or lower part is cut out into fringes and Garnished with Porcupine. The skins are joined below as high as the Ribs where an aperture is left on each side to suckle the child. The sleeves are joined to the body of the shirt on the shoulders only and encircle the arm from elbow to wrist, the upper part of the arm being covered only outside, but part of the leather is left to flap down so as to hide the pit of the arm." (Larocque, 1910, pp. 67–68).

We cannot be absolutely sure, but it is probable that Larocque was trying to describe a type of woman's dress worn by many other tribes of the Upper Missouri at that early period which was fundamentally a skin slip supported by straps over the shoulders, to which separate sleeves were added in cool weather to protect the wearer's arms from the cold. Certainly this garment, equipped with wrist length sleeves, tight fitting below the elbow, was quite different from the typical Crow woman's dress of a quarter of a century later portrayed by Catlin in 1832. (See Denig, 1953, Plate 4). That dress composed of two large animal skins (one forming the front and the other the back of the garment) with the tail projection hanging below the neck as an ornament and a cape-like insert over the shoulders and extending to about the wearer's elbow, had no true sleeves.[8]

Denig, writing in 1854, observed that Crow women "pay little attention to dress of any kind in their ordinary daily life" but "some of them have very handsome dresses which they wear on several occasions." (Denig, 1953, p. 34). The common winter dress of buffalo cowskin was undecorated. But a fine winter dress of bighorn skins "trimmed with scarlet and velvet and ornamented with porcupine quills" was valued at 3 buffalo robes or $9.00 in *ca.* 1850.

[8] This type is described and pictured in Wissler, 1915A, p. 65 and Fig. 16.

14

(Denig, 1930, p. 588). At that time the common summer dress of Crow women was of blue or green cloth and was valued at only $6.00. But a fancy summer dress, "a fine white bighorn skin cotillion adorned with 300 elk teeth," was worth 25 buffalo robes or $75. (*Ibid.*, p. 587).

It was not the basic material but the profusion of elk teeth employed in the decoration of these fancy dresses that made them so valuable. Only the lower incisors of the elk were sewn to these garments, and a hundred of them were worth the price of a pack horse, or about $20. (Kurz, 1937, p. 252). Kurz understood that the use of elk teeth for dress decoration originated among the Crow Indians. (*Ibid.*, p. 251). This is most probable in view of the fact that elk were more numerous in the Crow country than in other areas of the Upper Missouri region, and of the widely recognized reputation of the Crow Indians as the best dressed Indians of that region.

On January 7, 1852 Kurz drew the pencil sketch of two Crow women who were visiting Fort Union which is here reproduced as Fig. 13. The woman on the right wears a short-sleeved dress decorated on the back (and almost certainly on the front also) with large numbers of elk teeth. The one at the left wears a short-sleeved dress (probably of trade cloth) ornamented with a v at the neck and a band at the shoulder in quillwork or beadwork.

Fancy dresses worn by the wives of Crow chiefs who accompanied their husbands to Washington in 1873 appear to have been of a pattern which combined features of the two dresses pictured by Kurz two decades earlier. Elk teeth were sewn to the basic cloth material, and a narrow band of beadwork outlined an area of the upper portion of the garment extending over the shoulders and below the neck in a v-shape.[9]

Cloth dresses ornamented with elk teeth and some beadwork in this manner appear in numerous field photographs taken on the Crow Reservation in the succeeding half century. An example appears in the full-length portrait of White Hip's wife published in Lowie, 1922A, Fig. 14.

A dress of this type is here reproduced as Fig. 14. It was obtained from Mrs. Bull Tail by Wildschut in 1923. (CAT. 12/6406 MAIHF). This garment is of red flannel with a top insert of green flannel which is bordered with a narrow, continuous band of light blue seed beads, $\frac{1}{4}$" wide sewn in place by the lazy stitch. There

[9] Bureau of American Ethnology, Negatives 3,379, 3,380.

are also banded borders of green flannel at the ends of the sleeves
and the bottom of the dress. The dominant garment decoration,
however, is not the beadwork but the hundreds of imitation elk
teeth carved of bone which were individually tied to the surface
of the dress with cords. At that time these imitations had largely
replaced elk teeth for the decoration of women's dress due to the
scarcity of real incisors.

In the 1920s some Crow Indian women wore buckskin dresses
on festive occasions. These dresses were beaded in floral designs
similar to those used to decorate men's vests and leggings.

LEGGINGS

In 1805 Larocque observed that Crow women wore leggings
"reaching from the middle of the thigh with a garter below the
knees" and that "the seams of their leggings are covered with
blue beads (which is the kind they are most fond of)." (Larocque,
1910, p. 67).

The beaded field which covered the legging seam must then
have been a vertical band extending up the outside of the center
of the leg. This pattern of legging decoration appears to have pre-
vailed in the middle of the century, if we may judge from the
appearance of the legging worn by the woman at the right in Kurz'
drawing shown in Fig. 13.

However, the leggings worn by Crow women on dress occasions
in the Reservation Period were of a different pattern, possessing
wide cuffs at the bottom which were solidly beaded. The design
field was a horizontal rather than a vertical one. One of a pair of
women's leggings, collected by W. J. Hoffman on the Crow Reservation in the spring of 1892, is shown in Fig. 15. (CAT. 154,357
USNM). The cuff is completely covered with seed beads in lavender,
light blue, dark blue, white, green, yellow and red colors. The
borders are white, applied in the lazy stitch. The central band and
flanking triangles are outlined with single strands of white beads
sewn in the overlaid stitch, while the larger areas of the background are applied in the modified lazy stitch. Above the cuff
three white-beaded triangles outline a fourth triangle of dark blue
trade cloth sewn to the red flannel background.

Edward Curtis, who studied Crow Indian culture in the field in
the early years of this century, was told that women's leggings
were formerly embroidered with a large star on each side directly

above the heel. (Curtis, Vol. 4, 1909, p. 22). However, Crow women's leggings of the present century not only lack these stars but the cuffs have been decorated in simpler designs than is illustrated by the leggings collected by Hoffman in 1892.

Fig. 16 portrays a small girl's legging (CAT. 11/5334 MAIHF) and a woman's legging (CAT. 11/7691 MAIHF), both of which were collected by Wildschut on the Crow Reservation in the early 1920s. The child's legging of dark green cloth is beaded on the 3" high cuff in 11 horizontal bands of seed beads applied in the modified lazy stitch. The center band is green and the colors read outward from it toward both top and bottom—light blue, red, green, dark blue and white. The woman's legging of faded pink cloth bears a cuff $7\frac{3}{4}''$ high, similarly beaded in horizontal bands of solid colors, 16 in number.

In the 1920s some women's leggings were decorated with floral designs in beadwork. A number of Crow women wore leggings similar to those shown in Fig. 11 of Lowie's *Crow Indian Art*, but these leggings were beaded by Sioux, not by Crow, craftswomen.

BELTS

Traders furnished the Crow Indians with broad, thick, commercial leather belts which the women proceeded to embellish with seed beads. Such a belt was worn by a Crow woman who was photographed by Stanley J. Morrow in *ca.* 1879. (Hurt and Lass, 1956, Fig. 68). In the early years of this century beaded commercial leather belts were worn by both men and women on dress occasions. An example from the collections of this museum is pictured in Fig. 17. (CAT. 18/4758). It is $44\frac{1}{2}''$ long, $2\frac{3}{4}''$ wide and more than $\frac{1}{8}''$ thick. It is beaded throughout its length save for the $7\frac{1}{4}''$ at one end which was hidden from view when the belt was wrapped around the wearer's body. The beadwork is divided into nine panels so that the fifth panel, with the cross in the center, can be worn at the center of the back, and the other panels are arranged to maintain symmetry in design as seen from either the right or left side of the wearer. The common Crow background color of light blue predominates, while lavender occurs as a background in the third and seventh panels. The beads were applied loosely so that when the belt is laid flat (as in the photograph) the work appears sloppy. But when the belt was wrapped around its wearer's waist the horizontal lines of beadwork were pulled taut.

Beaded belts with white backgrounds and elaborate spreading designs, such as the one illustrated in Fig. 16 of Lowie's *Crow Indian Art* were intrusive. Most of them were of Western Sioux origin.

ROBES AND BLANKETS

In 1805 Larocque observed that Crow Indian men wore buffalo robes as outer garments and that these robes were either painted with representations of the wearer's war exploits or "garnished with beads and porcupine quills over the seam." (Larocque, 1910, p. 67). The seam referred to extended the full length of the robe along its center. For convenience in handling heavy buffalo robes during the laborious processes of dressing them Crow women commonly cut them in half along the center line. After the two halves were properly dressed they were sewn together again with sinew thread. The Crow Indians preferred to cover this seam with a band of decoration.

Carl Bodmer's field sketch, reproduced as Fig. 1, portrays a man standing at the far right wearing a buffalo robe bearing a broad horizontal band, elaborated by a rosette, across the robe's central portion. The main decoration probably is in porcupine quillwork although the band may be bordered with trade beads. Probably this is the same type of robe decoration Larocque saw among the Crow a quarter century earlier. George Catlin possessed a Crow robe bearing both painted representations of war honors and a central band of quillwork with rosettes introduced at intervals along its length.[10]

In 1851 Rudolph Kurz described a Crow buffalo robe he had collected: "Across the middle of it runs a broad band, decorated with beads, porcupine quills, and tiny bells that hang from rosettes." (Kurz, 1937, p. 127). In mid-century Crow warriors were also wearing bright colored trade blankets "loaded with beads worked curiously and elegantly across them." (Denig, 1953, p. 35).

In museum collections are preserved a number of Crow Indian beaded strips such as were used to decorate trade blankets. These are the more recent counterparts of the quilled and beaded strips which Crow women applied to buffalo robes to hide the center seams as much as a century and a half ago. Two beaded strips from the collections of this museum are portrayed in Fig. 18. The shorter of these measures $57\frac{1}{2}''$ long and $5\frac{1}{2}''$ wide. The three ro-

[10] Catlin's pencil drawing of this robe appears in his *Souvenir of the North American Indians*, a sketch book in the New York Public Library.

settes are 6″ in diameter. (CAT. 16/7244). The other specimen (CAT. 5/8152) is 66″ long and 4⁷/₈″ wide. Its four rosettes are each 5″ in diameter. There can be no doubt that the general composition of these beaded strips was derived from the quilled strips elaborated with rosettes made by Crow women more than a century ago. These beaded specimens evidence typical Crow Indian designs and bead colors of the Reservation Period. Wildschut found a few robes of elkskin and a larger number of blankets, to which beaded strips of this kind were sewn, among the Crow in the 1920s.

At that time Crow Indians also owned a few elkskins embroidered with 25 to 35 narrow bands of beadwork extending nearly the entire length of the robes. A pleasing decorative effect was obtained by changing the colors of the beads in each band at regular intervals and by fastening colored horsehair or strands of dyed wool between sections of each band. The two buckskin straps by which the robe was tied around the wearer's neck were commonly attached to rather small beaded rosettes. An example of this decorative treatment of an elkskin is portrayed in Fig. 19. The specimen depicted was collected by Wildschut in 1924 from Big Medicine. (CAT. 13/2263 MAIHF). According to Crow tradition these narrow bands of beadwork sewn to a robe in the lazy stitch were modern renderings of a similar pattern of robe ornamentation in porcupine quills employed by the Crow Indians long ago.[11]

[11] In the 1920s the Crow Indians possessed some of the painted robes bearing designs such as were commonly painted on the women's robes of the Sioux. (See illustration in Wissler, 1904, Fig. 83). But the Crow Indians told Wildschut that painted robes of this kind were not made by the Crow. They were imported from the Sioux. The painted robe shown in Fig. 5 of Lowie's *Crow Indian Art* and reproduced as a frontispiece in Ewers' *Plains Indian Painting* was, therefore, not the work of a Crow artist. It is of interest to recall that Larocque noticed that Crow women's robes were "never painted." (Larocque, 1910, p. 68). Ewers' Assiniboin informants told him that that tribe had a definite belief that women's robes should not have painted designs on them.

MOCCASINS

Larocque observed that the moccasins worn by the Crow Indians in 1805 were "made in the manner of mittens having a seam round the outside of the foot only without pleat." (Larocque, 1910, p. 67). This contemporary evidence of a one piece, soft-soled Crow moccasin as the prevailing early type supports the traditions observed by both Curtis and Lowie fully a century later. (Curtis, Vol. 4, 1909, p. 22; Lowie, 1922A, p. 226). However, neither of these later investigators indicated when the change from soft-soled moccasins to ones with separate, stiff rawhide soles came about. Apparently this change occurred well within the lifetime of their informants, for Capt. W. P. Clark in the early 1880s observed that "the Crows make their moccasins of one piece sewed at the heel, though some have separate soles." (Clark, 1885, p. 259). Apparently the transition from soft- to hard-soled moccasins was taking place at that time among the Crow.

A pair of winter moccasins of buffalo hide, hair inside, collected by Wildschut is of the old style soft-soled pattern. The seam extends around the outside of the foot from a point part way back on the inside to the center of the heel and up the back of the heel. See Fig. 20. (CAT. 14/2122 MAIHF).[12]

Patterns of moccasin decoration which were developed in the period of soft-soled footgear survived among the Crow Indians into the present century. The earliest pattern of Crow moccasin decoration of which we have any definite record employed a combination of a rosette with a band to form a design having the general appearance of an inverted keyhole. This design was placed over the center of the vamp and covered only a portion of its surface. It was also employed by both the Blackfoot and Sioux tribes for decorating moccasins. Ewers found that women of both those tribes referred to the design as "round beadwork."

This motif appears on the moccasins worn by the standing man at the left in Bodmer's drawing of a group of Crow Indians in 1833 (Fig. 1), on the moccasins worn by the woman at the left

---

[12] It is noteworthy that the sacred moccasin bundle collected by Wildschut (CAT. 14/6472 MAIHF) contains a pair of moccasins of the old, side-seamed, soft-soled pattern.

in Kurz' sketch nearly two decades later (Fig. 13), and on the moccasins worn by Medicine Crow of the 1880 delegation to Washington (Fig. 2, second man from the left). The design still enjoyed some popularity among the Crow in the 1920s.

The design is well represented by the pair of hard-soled, Crow moccasins shown in Fig. 21 (CAT. 3/2925 MAIHF). The rosette, beaded in overlaid stitch, has the light blue background so common in Crow beadwork, with red center, dark blue blocks and yellow and white border. The stem section, outlined in white beads, has a lavender background with bars and triangles in green, white and metal beads. The beaded border of this pair of moccasins also appears to be a survival from the soft-soled moccasin period. Notice that it extends from the toe to the heel around the outside of the foot only, reminiscent of the course of the seam in the older soft-soled moccasin pattern. This border is beaded in the lazy stitch in small right-angled triangles and transverse stripes.[13]

Figure 22 shows three hard-soled Crow moccasins collected by W. J. Hoffman for the U.S. National Museum in 1892. The one on the left is a woman's moccasin. (CAT. 154,354). The border was beaded in the lazy stitch in white with designs in dark blue, yellow and green beads. The solid-beaded vamp has designs in dark and light blue on a lavender background, beaded in the modified lazy stitch.

The full-beaded child's moccasin on the right (CAT. 154,356) bears four U-shaped designs on the vamp which the Indians commonly referred to as "horse tracks." Modifications of this design are portrayed in Fig. 23 on two moccasins collected by Wildschut three decades later. (CAT. 11/8006 and 11/8008 MAIHF, Fig. 23). The same designs appear on a pair of moccasins worn by Chief Short Tail Bull in a photograph taken on the Crow Reservation in ca. 1887.[14]

The floral beaded man's moccasin in the center of Fig. 22 is beaded in the overlaid stitch. (CAT. 154,355 USNM). All of the larger forms are outlined in white beads. The designs are in red, dark blue, light green, yellow, and lavender, the same combination of colors commonly used in the geometric beadwork of the Crow Indians during the Reservation Period. The growth in popularity of floral designs on moccasins in the late years of the nineteenth

---

[13] Another version of this pattern on a Crow moccasin appears in Lowie, 1922B, Fig. 18c.

[14] Neg. No. 104, 129 in The National Archives.

century and the early years of the present century paralleled the increasing use of floral beadwork among the Crow Indians in the decoration of men's vests, legging, gauntlets and women's leggings. Photographs of members of Crow delegations to Washington in 1873 and in 1880 show no moccasins bearing floral designs. Yet all three of the Crow chiefs who visited Washington in 1913 wore floral-beaded moccasins.[15]

In the early 1920s both geometric and floral designs appeared on the moccasins worn by Indians of this tribe. Fig. 24 illustrates eight moccasins of Crow make collected by Wildschut for this museum in 1923. Those appearing in the top row represent variations of a very popular Crow Indian moccasin design, consisting of an elaborated u-shape on the center of the vamp, without accompanying border. The details of these designs differ, but each is elaborated by two or more small double-triangles placed base to base, forming a motif commonly referred to as a 'feather design." On three of the four moccasins in the bottom row conventionalized floral elements have been substituted for the "feather designs." The fourth moccasin is beaded with a complex floral design in which geometric elements are entirely lacking.

In the 1920s Wildschut observed that women's and small children's moccasins were commonly beaded in horizontal bands across the vamps resembling the banded decorations on women's leggings. Narrow borders, completely encircling the entire moccasins above the sole seam were added.

During the early years of the present century the Crow Indians owned and wore many pairs of moccasins which had been received as gifts from other tribes. Of the 13 "Crow" moccasins illustrated in Lowie's *Crow Indian Art* only 4 appear to have been definitely of Crow origin. (Figs. 17a, 18a, 18c, and 20a). The other 9 moccasins were intrusive. Probably they were made by Sioux or Cheyenne women. Certainly none of them was of Blackfoot origin.

[15] Bureau of American Ethnology. Neg. 3430.

RIDING GEAR

Among the tribes of the Upper Missouri the Crow Indians were renowned as the richest in horses and the best horsemen. Charles Mackenzie, a Canadian trader who was at the Hidatsa villages on the Missouri when the Crow Indians came there to trade in 1805, remarked: "I was astounded to see their agility and address, and I do believe they are the best riders in the world." (Mackenzie in Masson, 1889, Vol. I. p. 345). Larocque, who had journeyed southward from the country of the Cree and Assiniboin, tribes poor in horses, was impressed by the fact that among the Crow "everybody rides, men, women and children." He further observed that Crow "women are indebted solely to their having horses for the ease they enjoy more than their neighbors." (Larocque, 1910, pp. 59, 64).

Our frontispiece shows clearly that when He-Who-Jumps-Over-Everyone dressed in his best clothes to visit the Hidatsa he ornamented his favorite horse no less elaborately than he did himself. Crow women also made colorful gear for their own horses so that they might look well on horseback on gala occasions.[16] The principal articles of decorated riding gear made and used by the Crow Indians were men's saddles and cruppers, and the saddles, head ornaments, collars, and cruppers placed upon women's horses.

SADDLES

Although most of the Crow men who visited the Hidatsa in the summer of 1805 rode bareback, others rode saddles which probably were of the type Kurz described nearly a half century later as constructed of "two leather cushions bound together by means of a broad solid leather girth." (Mackenzie, p. 345; Kurz, 1937, p. 260). Kurz' description of a mounted Crow warrior who came to Fort Union in January, 1852, mentioned that "his stirrups and saddle were also ornamented with beads and tassels." Fig. 25 reproduces Kurz' pencil sketch of a Crow Indian man's horse and its typical gear. The stirrups are not ornamented, but the skin pad saddle is

[16] See Lowie, 1922B, Fig. 12.

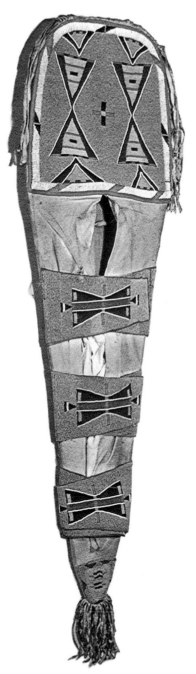

A CROW BEADED CRADLE
MAIHF CAT. NO. 8791, LENGTH, 46 IN.

decorated on one and probably both sides with a beaded rosette having a cross motif within it.

Women's saddles were of quite different construction. They had a wooden framework covered with rawhide, and high pommels and cantles flattened into large outward-extending ovals at their tops. Larocque was impressed by the height of the horns of the Crow women's saddles he saw in 1805, but he did not mention their decoration. (Larocque, 1910, p. 64). However, the artist Alfred Jacob Miller, in his description of the saddles of Indian women whom he met on the Sweetwater River in present Wyoming in 1837, noted that from the ends of the pommel and cantle "hang pendants made of brilliant colors, worked tastefully with beads and fringes." (Ross, 1951, p. 73).

Fig. 26 shows the beaded pendants which hang from the pommel and cantle of a Crow woman's saddle which was collected by W. J. Hoffman in 1892. (CAT. 154,368 USNM). The shapes of both flaps are the same and both are of red flannel, although the beaded designs upon them differ. The beadwork on the pommel pendant consists of a central field with light blue background, two A-shaped figures in contrasting colors (each bounded by a single line of white beads), narrow vertical borders of white beads, and a horizontal lower border in white, dark blue and lavender beads, from which are appended two small isosceles triangles in light blue, dark blue and white beads. All three typical Crow beadwork techniques appear on this flap—lazy stitch in the borders and small triangles, modified lazy stitch across the central area, and overlaid stitch in the fine-line borders of the A-shaped designs.

The cantle flap of this same saddle employs the same combination of techniques in a quite different design. The narrow vertical borders and the somewhat wider bottom one enclose a decorative field with a central cross on a light blue background which in turn is flanked by triangles in dark blue and red beads. On this pendant also lines of white beads set off the large central motif.[17]

The form of the rawhide-covered cottonwood stirrup used by Crow women probably is of Spanish derivation, but the beaded stirrup decoration is typically Crow Indian. Fig. 27 shows the stirrup of a Crow woman's saddle collected by Dr. R. B. Hitz in

[17] Although the beaded saddle pendants illustrated in Fig. 21 of Lowie's *Crow Indian Art* bear different designs, they are also of typical Crow workmanship.

Montana Territory and received by the U.S. National Museum 90 years ago (*i.e.* Oct. 23, 1868). It is CAT. 6,468. The bands beaded on the rawhide are in light blue; those on the red flannel flap are in light and dark blue, while the 3 small isosceles triangles are light blue. It is noteworthy that this may be the earliest documented use of seed beads by the Crow Indians. All of them are applied in the lazy stitch.[18]

HEAD ORNAMENTS

On gala occasions a Crow woman attached an elaborate, decorative pendant to the bridle of her riding horse. It extended from the horse's forehead over its face. Although we have seen no pictures of this ornament in use in earlier times, there are many field photographs which indicate its common use during the Reservation Period.[19]

A representative example of this ornament is shown in Fig. 28 (CAT. 2/4433 MAIHF). This specimen is 12″ high. It is composed of a cut rawhide base with a tab at the top for tying to the center of the forehead strap of a rawhide bridle, a beaded field, and border decorations of dyed and folded horse-hair (black and yellow) wrapped with colored yarn. The rosette portion of the beaded design bears a four-armed motif in light blue beads (with red center) which is outlined with white beads. The lower extension has a light blue beaded background within which appear two triangles one above the other in dark blue, yellow, red and green beads. The overall shape of the beaded area resembles that of the "round beadwork" pattern used by the Crow Indians in moccasin decoration.

HORSE COLLARS

The largest and most spectacular article of Crow Indian riding gear is the colorful collar which women placed on the neck of a favorite riding horse when they wished to dress it up for parades or other special occasions. Early examples of these collars are wanting, although Denig may have referred to their use prior to 1854 when he mentioned the "scarlet collars" on the horses of a

[18] A more elaborately beaded Crow stirrup is shown in Fig. 22 of Wissler, 1915B, p. 26.
[19] One of them appears in Fig. 12 of Lowie's *Crow Indian Art*.

Crow Indian camp on the march. (Denig, 1953, p. 35). Certainly the horse collars of the Reservation Period were most commonly beaded on a background of red flannel.

Plate 2 shows a fine example of one of these elaborate horse ornaments in full color. This specimen (CAT. 20/7717, MAIHF) was collected by Edward Borein, the artist. The long red-flannel side bands measure 42″ by 3¾″. The central panel is 10½″ square. The large hourglass figures and cross in the central panel may be seen on other examples of Crow horse collars in museum collections. So may the tall triangles one above the other separated by elaborated rectangles of other colors, which appear on the side bands. The principal differences are in the details of designs rather than in the primary composition of the decorative fields.[20]

George Catlin depicted a quill-decorated martingale on the horse ridden by He-Who-Jumps-Everyone which he saw in 1832. (See Frontispiece.) However, the large, beaded collars of the Reservation Period were placed only upon the horses of the women. Wildschut observed in the 1920s that no Crow woman would consider her riding horse fit to take part in a parade unless it wore one of these beaded collars.

CRUPPERS

The Frontispiece also portrays a broad, horse ornament which George Catlin described as "a most extravagent and magnificent crupper, embossed and fringed with rows of beautiful shells and porcupine quills of various colors." (Catlin, 1841, Vol. 1, p. 191). Two decades later Kurz drew a less elaborate crupper, decorated with cut fringes and two triangles (probably beaded) on a Crow Indian man's horse. See Fig. 25.

The crupper illustrated in Fig. 29 bears a close resemblance to the one sketched by Kurz and may date back to the 1870s or earlier. This specimen (CAT. 12/314 MAIHF) measures 32¾″ long. It consists of plain rawhide foresections (folded in the photograph) sewn to soft skin rear sections connected by a narrow skin band which passed under the horse's tail when the crupper was in use. The seams connecting the rawhide and soft skin pieces are covered with rectangular pieces of skin decorated with bands of beadwork in alternate red and blue colors. The soft skin areas are bordered

[20] A beaded horse collar in the Denver Art Museum has been described and pictured in great detail. (Douglas, 1937).

with blue beads with small isosceles triangles in the same color touching the borders. All the beads on this specimen are of the old pony bead size, and the technique of application is the lazy stitch.

The crupper commonly placed upon women's riding horses in the Reservation Period was of the type illustrated in Fig. 30. (CAT. 18/9233A MAIHF). The rawhide forepart of this crupper bears geometric designs painted in dark blue outlines. The triangles are filled with red and green painted areas and the backgrounds of the triangles are painted yellow. The rectangular cross pieces (hiding the seams) are beaded. The soft skin rear section is padded with a hair stuffing and its upper surface is decorated with beaded designs composed of tall isosceles triangles with smaller triangles at each corner.

Two Crow Indian cruppers in the U.S.National Museum which were collected by Hoffman in 1892 are of similar construction. The beaded designs on their soft skin sections are like those illustrated on the crupper just described.[21]

SADDLE BLANKETS

Prince Maximilian observed that "the haughty Crows rode on beautiful panther skins, with red cloth under them" when they visited the Hidatsa in the summer of 1833. (Maximilian, 1906, Vol. 22, p. 346). Nearly two decades later Kurz wrote that "the Crows never fail to use a piece of buffalo hide with hair, or some other skin as a saddle blanket." (Kurz, 1937, p. 260).

Although neither of these field observers mentioned the decoration of Crow saddle blankets with beads or porcupine quills, Kurz' drawing (our Fig. 25) portrays a saddle blanket, apparently of buffalo hide with the hair side next to the horse's body, decorated with a three diamonds over an hourglass shape in addition to five parallel horizontal bands near the rear corner. These designs may have been in beadwork.

In the early 1920s Wildschut found that beaded saddle blankets were not common among the Crow Indians. Those they made themselves were of dressed skin or heavy canvas bordered on three sides with beadwork. Narrow parallel stripes, similar to those used

[21] A similar crupper is portrayed in Wissler, 1915B, Fig. 14. Although labeled Shoshone, this specimen may be of Crow make. The crupper illustrated in Fig. 58 of Wissler's *Material Culture of the Blackfoot Indians* is not typical of the riding gear of those Indians. It, too, may be of Crow origin.

in decorating elkskin robes, sometimes were added as were small, oblong, beaded pendants sewn to the rear corners. Compared to the saddle blankets of the Sioux, which were bordered with broad bands of beadwork, those of the Crow Indians were quite simple affairs.

CONTAINERS

Like the other nomadic tribes of the Great Plains, the Crow Indians needed a variety of containers to carry their belongings when they moved camp as well as to store them inside their lodges when they encamped. Some of these containers were of tough rawhide and were decorated with painted geometric designs. Others, made of soft skins, were quill or bead decorated.

Beadwork was commonly used to decorate soft skin saddle bags, cases for weapons, cradles, tobacco pouches, mirror pouches, and containers for other small objects.

SADDLE BAGS

In his brief description of Indian women's riding gear, which he saw in 1837, Alfred Jacob Miller mentioned the "possible" sack "most elaborately worked in porcupine quills." (Ross, 1951, p. 73). The rectangular, top-opening "possible sacks" of the Crow Indians (so named because they served as containers for every possible thing from small trinkets to articles of clothing) were tied to women's saddles with buckskin cords. Wildschut learned that the Crow Indians formerly decorated these sacks with porcupine quills, but in his time they were beaded.

One of these handy containers appears in Fig. 31. (CAT. 18/4619 MAIHF). It measures $13\frac{1}{4}''$ wide and $8''$ high (with the flap closed). The surface of the side which was exposed to view when the sack was tied in place on a horse was decorated with six parallel bands of seed beads in the lazy stitch, resembling the beaded bands on elkskin robes. Each band is but 9 beads wide. A similar band follows the border of the flap, on which are mounted four small isosceles triangles. A broader band of beadwork covers each end of the sack. Typical Crow bead colors are used—blues, red, yellow, green and white.

"Possible sacks" of larger size and quite different decoration were made by the Western Sioux and neighboring tribes. The outer surfaces of many of them were completely covered with bead-

work applied in the lazy stitch. Two of these are illustrated in
Lowie's *Crow Indian Art*. They are not Crow, but Sioux "possible
sacks."

While he was at Fort Clark near the Mandan and Hidatsa villages in 1833, Carl Bodmer made a watercolor drawing of a handsome Crow Indian quiver. A reproduction of the lithograph made
from Bodmer's drawing appears in Fig. 32. An examination of the
artist's original watercolor reveals that the two large rosettes were
quilled, the central cross in orange and the background in natural
color quills. The two small rosettes, however, were beaded with
blue beads. The shoulder strap was not decorated.

Later the Crow Indians became renowned for their elaborately
decorated quiver straps. Capt. W. P. Clark, in describing Plains
Indian quivers in 1884, wrote:

"Extremely handsome ones are made by the Crows, mainly of
otter, and that portion of the strap by which the quiver is carried,
passing across the breast, being heavily beaded and fringed with
ermine. This particular style of quiver is as much a specialty
of the Crows as the blanket is of the Navajos." (Clark, 1885,
p. 313).

Thirty-two years earlier Kurz observed that the broad bands
by which the Crow warriors swung their bows, quivers and rifles
across their shoulders were decorated with beadwork. (Kurz, 1937,
p. 251). The band passing around the body of the young man on
the right in Kurz' drawing, reproduced as Fig. 7, probably is one
of these elaborately beaded straps. A similar strap for a gun case
appears in the same artist's sketch of a Cree Indian. It may have
been of Crow workmanship. (*Idem.*, Plate 30).

Our Fig. 33 shows a beautiful otter skin quiver collected by
Capt. Charles A. Bendire at Crow Agency, and accessioned by the
U.S. National Museum, July 7, 1892. (CAT. 164, 826). The broad
carrying strap of otter skin is decorated with a red flannel pendant
22" long and 6½" wide at the base which is completely covered
with beadwork in typical Crow designs, techniques and colors.
Both light blue and lavender backgrounds are used in different
segments of the decorative field. A smaller beaded flannel pendant
is attached to the strap and the base of the quiver is wrapped in
red flannel which is almost completely covered with beadwork.

GUN CASES

Although the Crow Indians possessed several hundred guns in 1805, the decorated gun case, which came to replace the quiver for bows and arrows, was not mentioned in the early literature on this tribe.

An attractively beaded gun case, collected by Major James M. Bell among the Sioux on Poplar River, Montana, was received at the U.S. National Museum in 1894. (CAT. L75). However this specimen, illustrated as Fig. 34, bears typical Crow beadwork. This fringed buckskin case, 44″ in length, has a red flannel wrapping at the barrel end which is beaded in conventional Crow fashion with narrow white borders and a light blue background separated from the large, triangular design of lavender, yellow and dark blue beads, by a line of white beads. The stock end is strikingly decorated with narrow white borders and hourglass shapes sewn to the red flannel so as to leave bright red triangles and a diamond area unbeaded. The Crow technique of the modified lazy stitch as well as both the lazy stitch and the overlaid stitch were used in beading this gun case.

SWORD AND LANCE CASES

The very elaborately decorated rawhide cases used by Crow Indians for carrying swords and lances on horseback received no mention in the early literature. However, Denig wrote that the Crow woman carried her husband's "sword, if he has one" which "is tied along the side and hangs down" when she moved camp on horseback. (Denig, 1953, p. 36).

A handsome scabbard of rawhide, collected by the artist, Edwin W. Deming, is shown in Fig. 35 (left). It is CAT. 8480 MAIHF. The scabbard contains a military sabre stamped "U.S. 1864," and bears the initials of the inspector, "CW." The case for this weapon is made of two pieces of rawhide cut into a form resembling that of a spade with a handle. The two pieces of rawhide, each 45″ long, were sewn together with buckskin cord and edged with red flannel. The narrow (or handle) portion is decorated with tall triangles and transverse bars in a technique rarely found on Plains Indian specimens. The outlines of the forms were incised with a sharp knife and the surface of the hide was scraped away within the area of these cuts, causing the decorations to be lighter in color than is the unscraped hide surface surrounding them.[22] Two beaded pendants of red flannel are tied to the handle portion, while the spade shape at the bottom is covered with red flannel elaborately beaded with a border of white beads broken by dark blue stripes, a background of light blue beads and designs in dark blue, yellow, red and green. The major forms are separated by a line of white beads.

A lance case of the same general form, collected by Edward Borein, appears on the right in Fig. 35. (CAT. 20/7709 MAIHF). It differs from the sword scabbard primarily in the fact that the narrow shaft portion of the rawhide is painted a dark blue leaving the tall triangles unpainted, achieving an effect in paint somewhat similar to that of the scraped design against a darker background appearing on the sword scabbard. Otherwise this specimen differs only in the details of the beadwork from the sword case beside it.

Maximilian observed that mounted Crow warriors carried lances "merely for show" in their impressive mounted maneuvers during their visit to the Hidatsa in the summer of 1833. (Maximilian, 1906, Vol. 22, p. 349). In the Reservation Period this relic of primitive warfare was carried in a rawhide scabbard of the type above described only by women in mounted parades. The scabbard was attached to the right side of the woman's saddle.[23]

CRADLES

Edwin T. Denig, in his description of a Crow Indian camp on the march, written in 1854, stated:

"It is often a strange and barbarous sight to see small children but a few days old tied to a piece of bark or wood and hung to the saddle bow which flies up at each jump of the horse when on the

---

[22] This same technique was employed in decorating the rawhide portion (which is all that remains) of an old Crow crupper in the collections of the museum. (CAT. 1/751 MAIHF). It was also used in decorating a rawhide parfleche in the Denver Art Museum which has been described and pictured by Douglas (1938). Although both of these specimens appear to be old, it would be difficult to believe that this type of ornamentation was employed before the Indians had access to sharp metal trade knives. Perhaps it was influenced by Spanish methods of decorating leather.

[23] A lance appears in an upright position on the right side of the decorated woman's horse pictured in Lowie's *Crow Indian Art*, Fig. 12. The scabbard is not visible. One of two other Crow lance cases in the collections of this museum was collected by Wildschut as recently as 1923.

3

gallop, their heads exposed to the hot sun or cold." (Denig, 1951, p. 37).

This fragmentary description might suggest that the elaborate cradle in use among the Crow Indians in the Reservation Period developed from a simpler form in common use more than a century ago. Many Crow cradles, collected since 1890, are preserved in museum collections. They are among the most highly decorated objects in Crow material culture.

These cradles consist of a flat board about 40" long and 11" to 12" wide at the broadest point near the top, tapering almost to a point at the bottom. The cradle board is covered with soft-dressed buckskin (or canvas) stretched tightly across the back with a loose pocket in the center of the front which provides both a hood for the baby's head and a covering for its body. When placed inside this pocket the child is held firmly in place by three pairs of broad straps. One pair crosses the baby's chest just under the armpits; another crosses his waist, and the third holds his ankles in place. These straps and the large, flat surface of the board above the baby's head are covered with beadwork. On some cradles the narrow, curved section of the cradle below the baby's feet is also beaded.

Women took great pains in beading their babies' cradles. These articles exemplify Crow beadwork at its best. A handsome Crow cradle from the Keppler Collection appears in full color in Plate 3. (CAT. 8791 MAIHF). It portrays clearly the effective contrast of the light blue beaded background favored by the Crow with the buckskin background of the cradle cover and with the large, angular beaded designs in contrasting colors. Notice again the use of white bead outlines for the major design motifs so commonly found in Crow beadwork.

Fig. 36 portrays three other Crow Indian cradles. In each of them the details of the beadwork differ, but all make use of typical Crow designs, beadwork techniques and colors. Fig. 36A, which bears the simplest design, is also probably the oldest of the three cradles shown. It was collected on the Crow Reservation by W. J. Hoffman in 1892. (CAT. 154, 361 USNM). The large inverted U-shaped area at the top of the cradle bears a light blue background within a narrow border of white and blue beads. The large diamonds are in dark blue and the crosses in red with green centers against yellow backgrounds. Each of the six straps is beaded in the same pattern (as was customary in Crow cradle decoration).

Each is divided into blocks of color (two of light blue and one of lavender in the center) by red, white and dark blue stripes. All three techniques commonly employed in Crow beadwork appear on this cradle.

The other cradles illustrated in Fig. 36B and C, show different designs employed in Crow beadwork. In Fig. 36B (CAT. 14/821 MAIHF) the background of the large field at the top is in lavender beads. However, in Fig. 36C (CAT. 2/3140) the more common light blue background was used.

BELT POUCHES

In the winter of 1851–52 Rudolph Kurz saw a young Crow warrior at Fort Union who carried a shot pouch with cover attached to the front of his belt and a second pouch, closed with a long tapering cover, fastened to the back of his belt. Both pouches were "absolutely covered with beads." (Kurz, 1937, pp. 259–260). On December 21, 1851, artist Kurz drew the pencil sketches of two Crow belt pouches which we have reproduced in Fig. 37. Apparently both of these pouches were beaded in geometric patterns on their long, triangular covers.

Crow men in the Reservation Period commonly used a belt pouch of different shape. The type is shown in Fig. 38. This pouch was collected by Hoffman in 1892 and was identified by him as "a bag for papers" (CAT. 154, 344 USNM). It is made of commercial leather with belt loops at the back and measures 5" high by 4⅝" wide at the top. This type of commercial leather pouch closely resembles the form of the percussion cap pouch issued to soldiers of the U.S. Army prior to the Civil War. The pouch may have been among the Army surplus items issued to the Crow Indians by the Government. But the beaded decoration on the cover was added by Crow Indian women. The background is again of light blue beads; the five-pointed star is outlined in dark blue and filled in with yellow beads enclosing a red circle. The narrow border is in alternate sections of red and green beads.

This form of belt pouch appears in photographs of Crow Indians taken in the field and others of Crow delegates to Washington in the early years of this century. The pouch was worn at the front of the body, attached to a broad, beaded leather belt. It served as a purse. The covers of the pouches pictured were beaded in floral designs.

3*

RATION TICKET POUCHES

Fig. 38 also shows another type of small pouch which was very useful to the Crow Indians. It was also collected by Hoffman on the Crow Reservation in 1892. (CAT. 154, 345 USNM). The back of this flat pouch is of soft buckskin, the front of stiff rawhide. It measures $4\frac{1}{2}''$ high and $2\frac{5}{8}''$ wide, just large enough to hold one of the cardboard ration tickets which were issued to Crow Indian family heads following the extermination of the buffalo. The Indians were warned not to lose their ration tickets, so they made pouches in which to keep them safely. And they proceeded to decorate these pouches with seed beads, on the front surfaces and the fold of the covers only. The background of this pouch is beaded in light blue, enclosing a dark blue outlined rectangle within which a red cross appears against a white background. Small blocks of dark blue beads were placed above and below the central rectangle. Yellow, dark blue and green beads appear in the narrow borders.

MIRROR POUCHES

When a Crow Indian man dressed to visit a trading post, to visit another tribe, or to take part in a parade or other festivity at home, he commonly carried over one arm a skin pouch containing his toilet articles—primarily a trade mirror, face paints and comb.

Rudolph Kurz' pencil drawing of Crow visitors to Fort Union in 1851 (our Fig. 7) shows one of these pouches suspended from the left wrist of the man on the left. The diamond and triangle designs appearing on this pouch are ones commonly employed by Crow beadworkers of later years in decorating broad, flat surfaces.

A Crow mirror pouch of more recent make is shown in Fig. 39. (CAT. 20/2871 MAIHF). It measures $3\frac{3}{4}''$ wide by $8''$ high. Both surfaces of this flat pouch are beaded with typical Crow Indian designs with narrow borders, lavender beaded backgrounds, and geometric forms. The arm strap, $2\frac{1}{2}''$ wide, is of figured cloth covered with red flannel on which appear blocks of beadwork in different colors outlined with white beads, and tall white hourglass forms. All three of the characteristic Crow beadwork techniques were used in decorating this pouch.[24]

[24] White Hip carries a mirror pouch over his left wrist in the photograph reproduced in Lowie, 1922A, p. 227. The visible side of this pouch is decorated in typical Crow designs—diamonds and tall triangles.

PIPE AND TOBACCO POUCHES

The traditional container for a Crow man's pipe and tobacco was the dressed skin of an animal. The small fawn skin of a deer, elk or antelope was preferred. In the Reservation Period the skin of a lamb was sometimes used. After the skin was dressed it was sewn up to make a sack with an opening at the head end sufficiently large to permit a man to insert his hand. This sack was closed by a buckskin thong wrapped around the neck of the skin and tied.

Some of these pouches were undecorated. Others were quilled or beaded. The eye holes were decorated with small copper discs or large, dark blue beads. Each of the four legs were wrapped for a distance of 2 or 3 inches with quills or strung beads. When beads were used for these wrappings each two rows were composed of a different color of beads—blue, red, yellow and white being most common. The animal's tail was similarly decorated and strips of red flannel were sewn to the ends of the legs and to the animal's nose.

Elderly Crow Indians told Wildschut that this type of pouch had been used by members of their tribe for many generations. In the early 1920s it was still preferred by the conservative old men of the tribe.

For special occasions, however, such as parades, celebrations and other festivities, when the Crow Indians changed from their drab "citizen's dress" to picturesque Indian costume in the Reservation Period, they carried more elaborately decorated pipe and tobacco pouches. They were valued as much for their decorative qualities as for their function as containers. Some of these pouches were of Crow make. But many others were obtained from neighboring tribes.

The two sides of a typical pipe and tobacco pouch of Crow Indian make are illustrated in Fig. 40. (CAT. 2/9637 MAIHF). The total height of this specimen measures 28", included the four-eared, beaded pouch and the long cut fringes below it which are strung with transparent basket beads and dew claws. Although the designs on the two sides of the pouch differ they are all ones occurring on other types of articles beaded by Crow Indian women. The techniques of bead application are those commonly used by the Crow, and the bead colors are ones frequently appearing in the beadwork of that tribe—light blue backgrounds, white outlining of hourglass forms, dark blue, red, yellow and green beads in the designs.

Other pipe and tobacco pouches made by Crow women differed in that the top of the pouch was cut in a straight line and bordered with a band of beadwork about $\frac{1}{2}''$ wide, and the buckskin fringes were wrapped for two to four inches of their upper portions with porcupine quills or colored yarn.

During the Reservation Period the Crow Indians received many pipe and tobacco pouches as gifts from neighboring tribes. And many of these pouches of alien make, but collected on the Crow Reservation, have passed into the possession of museums and have been recorded as Crow tobacco pouches. Some of these pouches were made by the Cheyenne, a few by the Blackfoot, but the great majority were of Teton Dakota (Western Sioux) origin.

Wildschut showed the illustrations of tobacco pouches in Lowie's *Crow Indian Art* (Figs. 6, 7, 8) to a considerable number of Crow Indian informants. All of them agreed that none of the 13 specimens illustrated was made by a Crow Indian. Crow women did not make pouches with broad sections of porcupine quill-wrapped rawhide slats between the pouch proper and the long, buckskin fringes, or with the entire backgrounds of the side panels beaded in narrow bands in the lazy stitch. Nor did the Crow bead-workers employ the complicated geometric designs appearing on the tobacco pouches illustrated in Lowie's study.

That the introduction of tobacco pouches from other tribes must have begun about 80 or more years ago is proven by the pouch carried in the hands of the standing man in Indian costume appearing in the photograph of the Crow delegation to Washington of 1880. (See Fig. 2). That pouch is definitely of an intrusive type. The popularity of these alien pouches is evidenced in many field photographs taken on the Crow Reservation since 1887. Examination of these photographs suggests that the pouches made by Dakota women were more common among the Crow than were those of their own creation. However, a tobacco pouch collected by W. J. Hoffman on the Crow Reservation in 1892, is definitely of Cheyenne type and probable origin. (CAT. 154, 328 USNM).

CHARACTERISTICS OF
CROW INDIAN BEADWORK

hree factors make the identification of Crow Indian beadwork less difficult than is the recognition of the beadwork of most other Plains Indian tribes. Crow beaders employed an unusual combination of embroidering techniques, as well as distinctive combinations of design elements and colors in their craftwork.

William C. Orchard described only two methods of sewing beads to broad surfaces of skin or cloth in use among the Plains Indians. However, Crow women very commonly employed three techniques in beading a single article.

Fig. 41 A shows one of these techniques, which Orchard termed the *overlaid* or *spot stitch*. (Orchard, 1929, pp. 128–129). In this technique the beads were threaded on sinew or thread and laid in the desired position, following the lines of the pattern. Then, with a second thread, the rows of beads were sewn securely in place by taking an overlaid stitch between every two or three beads. This held the beadwork close to the base material and gave a flat effect to the finished work. Blackfoot craftswomen employed this stitch almost exclusively in their beadwork produced during the Reservation Period. But Crow women used the *overlaid* or *spot stitch* primarily in beading curved lines (such as appeared in rosettes and in the outlines of floral designs), and in sewing down the single lines of white beads used to outline dark-colored designs.

Fig. 41 B illustrates a second beadwork technique which Orchard termed the *lazy stitch*. (Orchard, 1929, pp. 129–130). The beads were applied in a series of short, parallel rows, a single thread passing through the basic material at the ends of these rows only. This produced a ridged effect, the beads near the center of the rows tending to rise above the surface of the material, while those at the ends were held tight to it. This technique was widely

39

used by the tribes of the Upper Missouri in applying the large pony beads in common use among these Indians in pre-Reservation days. It remained the common method of applying beads of the smaller or seed bead size among the Sioux, Cheyenne and Arapaho beaders during the Reservation Period. However, Crow women of this more recent period used the *lazy stitch* primarily for narrow borders, small isosceles triangles, and for narrow bands of bead-work such as appear on the neck flaps of men's shirts, on cloth leggings, elkskin robes and "possible sacks." These bands usually measure less than one-half inch in width.

Fig. 41 C illustrates a third beadwork technique in common use among Crow beadworkers in the Reservation Period. The beads were placed upon the material in parallel rows and sewn down at the ends as in the "lazy stitch" beading. However, these rows of beadwork may measure three or more inches in length. To prevent the centers of these lines from sagging and hanging loose other threads are run at right angles to the rows of bead-work—under the first row and back over it, under the second and back, etc., in a series of back stitches. This technique was first described by Frederic H. Douglas in a detailed analysis of a single Crow Indian specimen, a beaded horse collar. (Douglas, 1937, p.6). Examination of a large series of Crow specimens shows that it was a common Crow beadwork technique. We have termed this comb-ination of the *lazy stitch* and back stitch the *modified lazy stitch*. However, since it was first described in an analysis of a Crow beaded artifact, and since it was widely used in Crow beadwork it could just as properly be termed the *Crow stitch*.

Crow Indian women employed it in the beading of broad back-grounds of solid colors, as well as in beading the filler colors in large geometric and floral designs. The transverse lines of back-stitching were placed irregularly at intervals of from 6 to 12 or more beads. Thus in a row of beads $2\frac{1}{2}''$ long, appearing on a Crow legging, five backstitches were used to tie down the beads.

This technique appears on the majority of Crow beaded objects in the Hoffman Collection of 1892. It appears with equal common-ness among the beaded objects collected among the Crow Indians by Wildschut 30 or more years later.

The effect of this stitch upon the appearance of the beadwork varied. In the best Crow beadwork executed in this technique the beads lie nearly as flat as do beads applied in the overlaid stitch. However, when the work was carelessly done or when the transverse lines of backstitching were too widely separated the beaded rows tended to hang loose and to give the design a rather sloppy appearance.[25]

BEADWORK DESIGNS

Although Crow Indian women very rarely produced two pieces of beadwork which were identical in every detail, they showed a marked tendency to employ a limited number of design elements in their geometric beadwork. Fig. 42 illustrates 15 design elements employed repeatedly in Crow Indian beadwork.

Fig. 42A represents a long narrow band of a single color of beads but varying in length and width with the particular circumstances of its use. It occurs commonly on articles of men's and women's clothing, on riding gear and on containers. Not only does it appear frequently as a narrow border for a large decorated field but on some articles it is *the* major beaded design element. See the beaded panels of the man's shirt in Fig. 4, the women's dress in Fig. 14 and the women's leggings in Fig. 16.

Fig. 42B is a long narrow band divided into rectangular blocks of a single color of beads by transverse stripes beaded in other colors. These stripes vary in width. This element appears in narrow borders, but it also may be the primary design element on some beaded articles. See the man's war shirt in Fig. 3, the shirt panels and fan in Fig. 11, the neck flaps of the men's shirts in Figs. 4 and 5, the beaded robe in Fig. 19, and the saddle bag in Fig. 31. Not uncommonly a band of this kind was employed to divide a decorative field into two bilaterally symmetrical areas, as illustrated by the man's shirt panels in Fig. 5, the man's legging in Fig. 8, the woman's legging in Fig. 15, the beaded cradle straps in Plate 3, the upper beaded area of the cradle in Fig. 36c, and the tobacco pouch in Fig. 40.

Fig. 42C is a variation of 42B in which the stripes run diagonally rather than at right angles to the length of the band. It appears less commonly than 42B in border decorations. Examples may be seen on the cradle in Plate 3, the moccasin in Fig. 22 (left), and the tobacco pouch, Fig. 40. It is also found occasionally within the principal design fields as illustrated by the man's legging in Fig. 10, the belt in Fig. 17, and the blanket strip (Fig. 18).

[25] We are indebted to Margaret E. Ewers for her analysis of the beadwork techniques used on the Crow specimens in the W. J. Hoffman Collection.

Fig. 42D is a small isosceles triangle, either in solid color or subdivided by a narrow horizontal stripe of another color. The apex of this triangle touches a band of beadwork or the angle of a much larger triangle. This design element appears on a wide variety of articles in Crow beadwork. See the men's shirts in Figs. 3 and 5, the men's leggings in Figs. 7 and 10, the child's moccasin in Fig. 22, the pommel and stirrup ornaments in Figs. 26 and 27, the cruppers (Figs. 29 and 30), the saddle bag (Fig. 31), the cradle straps in Plate 3, and the tobacco pouch in Fig. 40. Crow beadworkers seemed to have a particular fondness for this little triangular design element.

Fig. 42E is a nearly equilateral triangle, usually but not always beaded in a single color, and less than 2" high. Although this element occurs less frequently on other beaded articles, it appears commonly in the decoration of the brow bands of Crow feather bonnets. (See Fig. 12). It also may be seen on the flannel background of the woman's legging in Fig. 15, the moccasin in Fig. 21 and the horse head ornament in Fig. 28.

Fig. 42F is a small, right-angled triangle which stands on its broad base. The right angle may be either at the left or the right. In some designs these triangles appear one above the other as in the beaded legging panel in Fig. 8. In others they are placed in a row as in the beaded quiver in Fig. 33. While in moccasin borders these triangles may have their bases on the outside of the border or they may be inverted. (See Figs. 21 and 23, right).

Fig. 42G is an isosceles triangle having a wide angle at the top and a broad base. Two pairs of these elements appear on the beaded leggings worn by the man at the far left in the photograph of the Crow delegation of 1880. (Fig. 2). These are prominent elements in the decoration of the man's shirt panels in Fig. 5, and the woman's legging in Fig. 15. They also appear on the gun case in Fig. 34, the scabbards in Fig. 35, and the cradle straps in Fig. 36, right, as well as in the moccasin border in Fig. 22, right.

Fig. 42H is a small diamond-shaped element composed of two tall triangles, each of a different color beads, with coinciding bases. This element was commonly known to the Upper Missouri tribes as a "feather design." Crow beaders made little use of it save in the decoration of moccasins. (See Fig. 24). They may have borrowed this design from the Sioux or Assiniboin who made much more common use of it in their beadwork.

Fig. 42 I consists of four rectangular blocks of the same color of beads surrounding a rectangle beaded in a contrasting color. This element appears on the shirt worn by Plenty Coups in 1880 (Fig. 2, second man from right), on a moccasin collected a decade later (Fig. 22, left), on a moccasin obtained by Wildschut three decades after that (Fig. 24, second from right in top row), and on the panel at the base of the cradle in Plate 3.

Fig. 42 J is a rectangle outlined in solid color which contrasts with that of the rectangle. This element was worked in quills on the old leggings in Fig. 6, and in beads on the leggings worn by Pretty Eagle of the 1880 delegation. (Fig. 2, far right). It also appears on the ration ticket pouch collected in 1892. (Fig. 38).

Fig. 42 K is a blocky cross. Usually the arms of the cross are beaded in one color enclosing a central square of a contrasting color. The cross appears as the central figure in the beadwork on a variety of articles. See the arm panel of the shirt drawn by Bodmer in 1833 (Fig. 1, left), the longer of the two blanket strips in Fig. 18, the cantle pendant of the woman's saddle in Fig. 26, the center panel of the horse collar in Plate 2, the base of the scabbard in Fig. 35, right, the upper panels of three of the four cradles illustrated in Plate 3 and Fig. 36, as well as the straps of two of these cradles, and the ration ticket pouch in Fig. 38. Crosses also appear as decorative elements on the belt in Fig. 17, and the quiver in Fig. 33. Variants of the cross occur in the centers of rosettes, as illustrated by the chest ornament in Bodmer's drawing (Fig. 1), the pad saddle rosette sketched by Kurz two decades later (Fig. 25), and the horse head ornament of the Reservation Period. (Fig. 28).

Fig. 42 L is a large diamond outlined with beads in a contrasting color. It appears most prominently in the decoration of the cradle collected in 1892 (Fig. 36, left), the blanket strip (Fig. 18, lower), the lance scabbard (Fig. 35, right), and the tobacco pouch in Fig. 40. Notice that in the majority of these examples the cross element (Fig. 42 K) appears in the center of the diamonds. Tall diamonds without central crosses were sketched by Kurz in his pencil drawings showing a Crow saddle blanket and mirror pouch. (Figs. 7 and 25).

Fig. 42 M is a more complicated design consisting of a tall isosceles triangle which is commonly elaborated internally with smaller triangles or horizontal bands of beadwork. These tall triangles are prominent figures in the beadwork on horse collars

(Plate 2), cradles (Fig. 36, center), and quivers. (Fig 33). They also appear on a crupper and on the belt pouches pictured by Kurz. (Figs. 25 and 37).

Fig. 42N is an hourglass shape formed of two isosceles triangles joined at their apices. Some of these elements are quite large and are internally elaborated as are those appearing on the cradle in Plate 3. Others are in solid color such as those at the stock end of the gun case in Fig. 34. Mid-nineteenth century examples of the use of this element appear in Kurz' sketches of Crow leggings (Fig. 7), a saddle blanket (Fig. 25), and a belt pouch. (Fig. 37, left).

Fig. 42O is another hourglass shape in which the center is less constricted than in element 42N. It too is sometimes internally elaborated with horizontal bands and blocks of color as illustrated by the beading on the upper portion of the cradle (Fig. 36, right), or by a central lengthwise band as on the cradle straps in Plate 3. Two forms of this design appear on the flat side and on the carrying strap of the mirror pouch in Fig. 39. Other examples appear on the tobacco pouch in Fig. 40, left.

The rosette is the most common of the curvilinear designs in Crow beadwork. Beaded rosettes appear in combination with porcupine-quilled ones on the quiver drawn by Bodmer in 1833 (Fig. 32). One is shown on the pad saddle in Fig. 25. Rosettes also were prominent design elements in blanket strips (Fig. 18), horse head ornaments (Fig. 28), and in the "round beadwork" pattern of moccasin decoration. (Figs. 1, 2, and 21).

The U-shaped design, internally elaborated in various ways, was used by Crow beaders solely in the decoration of moccasin vamps. (Fig. 24).

Floral beadwork, including the conventionalized representation of leaves and stems as well as flowers, by Crow beaders cannot be differentiated from the floral beadwork of neighboring tribes with certainty in many cases. Among the Crow Indians floral patterns were used primarily in the decoration of articles of clothing and accessories, such as moccasins, leggings, vests, gauntlets and belt pouches. (See Figs. 11, 12, 22 and 24).

Although the simpler geometric elements used by Crow beaders also appear in the beadwork of other Upper Missouri tribes, the Blackfoot and Sioux of the Reservation Period commonly combined these designs with others which were not typical of Crow beadwork. The characteristic "mountain design" of the Blackfoot, a stepped triangle, appears so rarely in Crow beadwork that we may be justified in considering its use by Crow craftswomen as an example of borrowing from the Blackfoot. All Crow examples of its use are recent (*i.e.* twentieth century).

Such very common elements in Dakota beadwork since 1870 as the "twisted," "full-of-points," "forked tree," "dragon fly" and "arrow" designs reproduced in Wissler's *Decorative Art of the Sioux Indians* (Fig. 71) are lacking in Crow beadwork. The very elaborate Sioux geometric patterns combining solid, angular elements with fine lines illustrated in Lyford's *Quill and Beadwork of the Western Sioux* (Figures 28–46) are also wanting in the beadwork of the Crow Indians.

BEAD COLORS

The larger size of pony beads employed in the beadwork of the Upper Missouri tribes prior to the 1860s were available in a narrow range of colors—blue, white, black, red, and amber. The few documented examples of Crow beadwork of that period indicate a marked preference for blue beads.

However, a much wider range of bead colors became available in the smaller seed beads which entirely replaced pony beads in the Crow beadwork of the Reservation Period. Old bead sample cards used by traders prior to 1900 show more than 80 colors of seed beads from which Indian women could make selections. Nevertheless, Crow beaders generally employed only seven colors in their work and showed little disposition to experiment with different color combinations. Crow beadwork of the Reservation Period may be identified as readily from the colors employed as from the forms of the designs or the methods of sewing the beads in place.

The following are common color characteristics of Crow Indian beadwork:

1. The seven colors of beads commonly found in Crow beadwork of the Reservation Period are (roughly in order of the numbers of beads used) light blue, lavender, white, dark blue, red, yellow and green. Black or orange beads are very rarely found in examples of Crow beadwork.

2. Crow beadworkers showed a very marked preference for light blue backgrounds. Sometimes lavender backgrounds were sub-

stituted. But the white beaded backgrounds so common in Sioux beadwork are lacking in that of the Crow.

3. Crow beaders commonly used white beads in narrow borders of large design areas, but they used white beads sparingly in beading the larger design elements within these borders. However, they frequently outlined their larger design elements in a single line of white beads to set them off from their light blue or lavender backgrounds. Numerous examples of this latter use of white beads appear in the illustrations for this paper.

4. Crow beaders frequently used dark blue beads to outline the larger designs.

5. Red, yellow and green beads were used primarily for accents.

6. Trade cloth, preferably red flannel, was employed extensively as backgrounds for beaded designs in which few if any red beads were used.

SYMBOLISM IN CROW BEADWORK

Although Wildschut repeatedly questioned Crow Indians about the symbolism of their beaded designs he obtained but meagre information on the subject. It was his impression that by the 1920s tribal knowledge of the meanings of designs, if they ever did have symbolism, was lost.

However, some informants claimed that the number of horizontal bands of beadwork on a woman's leggings might represent the number of coups her husband had counted in battle; that the four feather designs on a man's moccasins signified that the wearer had counted the four major coups recognized by the Crow Indians; that horse tracks beaded on moccasins indicated that the wearer had captured horses from the enemy; and that the transverse stripes on men's shirts symbolized the coups they had counted. The beaded cross was said to represent the morning star.[26]

Wildschut's informants interpreted color symbolism as follows:

Red represented property, blood or desire for revenge.

Black (very rarely employed in Crow beadwork) symbolized revenge accomplished, or clouds.

White was emblematic of purity and also of hail and fog.

Green represented the earth.[27]

[26] Wissler found that Sioux men also tended to interpret the designs executed by women in terms of military symbolism. (Wissler, 1904 pp. 259 ff).

[27] Lowie found Crow design and color symbolism to be meagre and in most cases quite subjective. (Lowie, 1922B, pp. 319–320).

HISTORY OF CROW INDIAN BEADWORK

In reviewing the history of Crow Indian beadwork it is important to recognize that beadwork was but one of three major media employed by the women of that tribe in decorating articles of clothing, riding gear and containers. Although all three of these media—painting, porcupine quillwork, and bead embroidery—existed among these Indians at the time of François Larocque's earliest known description of Crow Indian culture in 1805, beadwork then must have been of relatively recent origin. The first embroidering beads probably were obtained by Crow craftswomen from neighboring tribesmen who had direct contacts with white traders. Probably these beads did not become available to the Crow women until the latter part of the 18th century. On the other hand, earth and vegetable pigments and porcupine quills, the basic materials employed in painting and quillwork, were plentiful in the Crow country. Painting and quillwork were aboriginal crafts. Their prior existence definitely affected the use of beads and beadwork design among the Crow Indians.

The history of Crow Indian beadwork appears to fall into two major periods. The first period extended from the beginning of the craft, some time prior to 1805, to about the middle of the 19th century. During this period beadwork was a decorative medium of secondary importance. Beads, in limited numbers, were used primarily for outlining or supplementing larger decorative areas worked in porcupine quills. This use is exemplified by the beaded and quilled leggings portrayed in Fig. 6 and the beaded and quilled Crow quiver drawn by Bodmer and reproduced as Fig. 32. Certainly when the Crow Indians were described by Catlin and Maximilian and pictured by Catlin and Bodmer in the early 1830s, quillwork was the major medium employed by the Crow craftswomen in decorating dress clothing and riding gear. A close examination of Catlin and Bodmer's original drawings and paintings indicates that this was also true of the decorative art of the Mandan and Hidatsa at that time. And Maximilian is our authority for the fact that some of the articles worn by those tribes at that time were actually obtained from the Crow.

Some of the simpler designs employed in Crow beadwork in more recent times appear to have been adopted from the earlier technique of porcupine quillwork. Among these are probably at least five of the elements pictured in Fig. 42, the narrow, solid-colored band (A), the band with transverse stripes (B), outlined rectangle (I), the outlined rectangle (J) and the cross (K). In addition the quilled rosette antedated the beaded rosette in Crow decorative art.

Undoubtedly these design elements also appeared in the quill-work of other Upper Missouri tribes of the early 1830s. In view of the paucity of documented specimens or other detailed information on the arts and crafts of the Upper Missouri tribes before 1832, it is impossible to determine which tribe originated any of these design elements in quillwork. However, in view of the high repu-tation of the Crow Indians for originality it is doubtful if the craftswomen of that tribe played a passive role in the develop-ment of these quillwork designs or in the adaptation of the designs to beadwork.

The second major period of Crow Indian beadwork began in the years between 1834 and 1850 and has continued into the present century. Early in this period beadwork came into its own as a major medium of decoration. Certainly by the time of Kurz, *i.e.* 1851–1852, beadwork had in large part supplanted quillwork as the dominant medium employed by Crow craftsworkers in deco-rating dress clothing, riding gear and containers. Quillwork con-tinued to decline in importance, and finally disappeared altogether. Although Wildschut learned that the last Crow Indian quillworker, the mother of Daylight, died in the month of June, 1922, very little quillwork had been done by members of the tribe since *ca.* 1890. It is probable that most of the quilled shirts and other quilled articles portrayed in photographs of Crow Indians taken since 1890 were made by the Sioux.

The designs appearing in Crow Indian beadwork of the Reser-vation Period, however, continued to show the influence of quill-work. Some of them also resembled closely the painted designs which Crow women applied to rawhide parfleches, bonnet cases, containers for medicine bundles and tipi door flaps. Unlike the beadwork of the Sioux and the Blackfoot of the Reservation Period, Crow geometric beadwork shows a close resemblance to the rawhide painting of the tribe. Compare the painted designs on the Crow parfleche collected by J. I. Allen prior to 1889 (CAT. 130,

4

574 USNM), and the painted headdress case (CAT. 20/7699 MAIHF), here reproduced as Figs. 43 and 44, with the triangular and dia- mond-shaped elements in Crow beadwork illustrated in Fig. 42. Compare them also with the photographs of cradles, the tobacco pouch and the mirror pouch in Plate 3 and Figs. 36, 39, 40, as well as with the belt pouches drawn by Kurz more than a century ago. (Fig. 37). Note how Crow craftswomen, many of whom were pro- ficient in both media, solved the problem of decorating a broad, flat surface in much the same way whether they were doing it with trade beads or paints. Still more striking is their similarity of treating the long, narrow beaded, side panels of horse collars (Plate 2), and the painted rawhide front sections of cruppers (Fig. 30), as well as the shafts of lance cases (Fig. 35, right) with tall triangles separated by bars. In these instances the shapes of the surfaces to be decorated rather than the media employed ap- peared to dictate the designs to be used. In view of the chrono- logical priority of painting as well as the greater ease with which designs could be painted, it seems reasonable to assume that these designs were first developed in painting and were adapted to beadwork.

The growing popularity of floral designs in Crow beadwork during the Reservation Period paralleled a similar trend toward floral design among the Blackfoot in the same period. Both tribes may have been influenced by the floral beadwork of the Cree Indians.

However, the many ethnological specimens bearing typical Sioux geometric designs beaded in the lazy stitch that have been collected on the Crow Reservation since 1890 do not indicate that Crow beadworkers copied Sioux beadwork. Rather these articles reached the Crow as gifts from the Sioux during the Reser- vation Period. After the intertribal wars among the Upper Mis- souri tribes ended in the middle 1880s, frequent visits were made between members of formerly hostile tribes. The Sioux had a strong motive for paying visits to the Crow. They had had most of their horses taken from them during their wars with the whites in the '70s. They knew that of all the tribes of the region the Crow were the wealthiest in horses. So they made repeated visits to the Crow to obtain horses. The great chief, Sitting Bull, accompanied one of these horse-seeking parties to the Crow Reservation in the late 1880s. (Vestal, 1957, pp. 251–254).

Having little else to offer the Crow Indians in exchange, the

Sioux gave them handsome articles of craftwork made by their women. Once friendly relations were established between these former enemies, repeated visits and exchanges of gifts followed. Thus the Crow Indians came into possession of numerous beaded vests, women's leggings, belts, moccasins, tobacco pouches and other articles made by the Sioux.

At the same time the Crow obtained beaded vests, moccasins, tobacco pouches, etc. from their former Cheyenne enemies who had been settled on a reservation adjacent to their own. In the 1890s the Crow exchanged visits with their former bitter enemies the Blackfoot tribes to the north and a similar exchange of gifts was inaugurated. Thus many traditional articles of Crow manufacture such as beaded men's suits, moccasins and various kinds of containers came into the possession of the Blackfoot and artifacts of Blackfoot origin passed into Crow ownership.

It is unfortunately true that most collectors among the tribes of the Upper Missouri were not aware of the extent of this thriving interchange of handicrafts among the tribes of the region. They assumed that an article collected on a reservation was made by the tribe of Indians residing there. Unfortunately for the record, many Indians preferred to sell collectors articles they had received as gifts from other tribes rather than those made by their own people. And when these specimens reached museums they were commonly accessioned as objects made by and representative of the crafts of the tribe residing on the reservation where they had been collected.

It is understandable, therefore, that studies of tribal styles based solely upon museum collections have served only to perpetuate the errors of identification appearing in museum records. Even such painstaking studies as Clark Wissler's *Distribution of Moccasin Decorations among the Plains Tribes* were distorted by the erroneous identifications of some of the specimens examined. The recent detailed study of Northern Plains Indian beadwork by the Science Museum of St. Paul, Minnesota, based entirely upon an analysis of museum specimens, has suffered from the same basic cause, an inability to verify the tribal origins of objects on the basis of museum records alone. (Powell, 1953).

The present study of Crow Indian beadwork should demonstrate that repeated analyses of museum collections are not enough to provide an adequate characterization and history of the beadwork of the Indian tribes of the Upper Missouri. Studies of museum

4*

specimens must be supplemented by and cross-checked with detailed studies of the literature and of the extensive pictorial record compiled by artists and photographers. And above all they should be augmented by intensive fieldwork among the Indians themselves. Plains Indian informants are still available whose memories and knowledge of the crafts of their respective tribes cover the period since *ca.* 1890, within which the great majority of handicraft specimens in our museum collections were obtained in the field.

BIBLIOGRAPHY

Catlin, George

1841. Letters and Notes on the Manners, Customs and Condition of the North American Indians. 2 Vols. London.

Chittenden, H. M., and Richardson, A. T. (editors).

1905. Life, Letters and Travels of Father Pierre Jean De Smet. 4 Vols. New York.

Clark, Capt. W. P.

1885. The Indian Sign Language. Philadelphia.

Curtis, Edward S.

1907–1930. The North American Indian. 20 Vols. Norwood, Massachusetts.

Denig, Edwin T.

1930. Indian Tribes of the Upper Missouri. Ed. by J. N. B. Hewitt. *46th Annual Report, Bureau of American Ethnology.* Washington.

1953. Of the Crow Nation. Ed. by John C. Ewers. *Anthropological Paper No. 33. Bulletin 151, Bureau of American Ethnology.* Washington.

Douglas, Frederic H.

1937. A Crow Beaded Horse Collar. *Material Culture Notes No. 2, Denver Art Museum.*

1938. An Incised Bison Rawhide Parfleche. *Material Culture Notes No. 6, Denver Art Museum.*

Ewers, John C.

1939. Plains Indian Painting. Palo Alto, California.

1945. Blackfeet Crafts. *Indian Handcrafts Series No. 9, U.S. Indian Service.* Lawrence, Kansas.

1954. The Indian Trade of the Upper Missouri before Lewis and Clark: An Interpretation. *Bulletin Missouri Historical Society*, Vol. 8. No. 1. St. Louis.

Gunther, Erna

1950. The Westward Movement of Some Plains Traits. *American Anthropologist*, Vol. 52. No. 2.

Hayden, Ferdinand V.

1862. Contributions to the Ethnography and Philology of the Indian Tribes of the Missouri Valley. *American Philosophical Society. Transactions.* n. s. Vol. 12, Part 2. Philadelphia.

Hurt, Wesley R., and Lass, William L.

    1956. Frontier Photographer. Stanley J. Morrow's Dakota Years. Lincoln, Nebraska.

Kroeber, Alfred L.

    1908. Ethnology of the Gros Ventre. *American Museum of Natural History. Anthropological Papers*, Vol. 1, Part IV. New York.

Kurz, Rudolph F.

    1937. Journal of Rudolph Friedrich Kurz ... 1846–1852. Ed. by J. N. B. Hewitt. *Bulletin 115, Bureau of American Ethnology*. Washington.

Larocque, François

    1910. Journal of Larocque from the Assiniboine to the Yellowstone. *Publication No. 3, Canadian Archives*. Ottawa.

Larpenteur, Charles

    1898. Forty Years a Fur Trader on the Upper Missouri. Ed. by Elliott Coues. 2 Vols. New York.

Lowie, Robert H.

    1922A. The Material Culture of the Crow Indians. *American Museum of Natural History. Anthropological Papers*, Vol. 21, Part III. New York.

    1922B. Crow Indian Art. *American Museum of Natural History. Anthropological Papers*, Vol. 21, Part IV. New York.

    1935. The Crow Indians. New York.

Lyford, Carrie A.

    1940. Quill and Beadwork of the Western Sioux. *Indian Handcrafts Series No. 1, U.S. Indian Service*. Lawrence, Kansas.

Mackenzie, Charles

    1889. The Missouri Indians, 1804–1805. In L. R. Masson, Les Bourgeois de la Compagnie du Nord-Ouest. Vol. 1. Quebec.

Mason, J. Alden

    1926. A Collection from the Crow Indians. *University of Pennsylvania Museum Journal*, Vol. 17. Philadelphia.

Maximilian, Alexander Philip, Prince of Wied Neuwied.

    1906. Travels in the Interior of North America. In Early Western Travels. Ed. by Reuben Gold Thwaites. Vols. 22–24. Cleveland.

Orchard, William C.

    1929. Beads and Beadwork of the American Indians. *Museum of the American Indian Heye Foundation, Contributions* Vol. XI.

Powell, Louis H.

    1953. A Study of Indian Beadwork of the North Central Plains. *Indian Leaflets No. 5–7, The Science Museum*, St. Paul, Minnesota.

Raynolds, W. F.
  1868. Report on Exploration of the Yellowstone River. Washington.

Ross, Marvin C.
  1951. The West of Alfred Jacob Miller. Norman, Oklahoma.

Vestal, Stanley
  1957. Sitting Bull Champion of the Sioux. Norman, Oklahoma.

Wissler, Clark
  1904. Decorative Art of the Sioux Indians. *American Museum of Natural History, Bulletin.* Vol. XVIII, Part III. New York.
  1910. Material Culture of the Blackfoot Indians. *American Museum of Natural History. Anthropological Papers,* Vol. 5. Part I. New York.
  1915A. Costumes of the Plains Indians. *American Museum of Natural History, Anthropological Papers,* Vol. 17. Part II. New York.
  1915B. Riding Gear of the North American Indians. *American Museum of Natural History, Anthropological Papers,* Vol. 17. Part I. New York.
  1927. Distribution of Moccasin Decorations among the Plains Tribes. *American Museum of Natural History, Anthropological Papers,* Vol. 29. Part I. New York.

Wood, W. Raymond
  1957. Perforated Elk Teeth: A Functional and Historical Analysis. *American Antiquity,* Vol. 22. No. 4.

FIGURE I

FROM A LITHOGRAPH AFTER CARL BODMER

CROW INDIANS NEAR FORT CLARK IN 1833

FIGURE 2

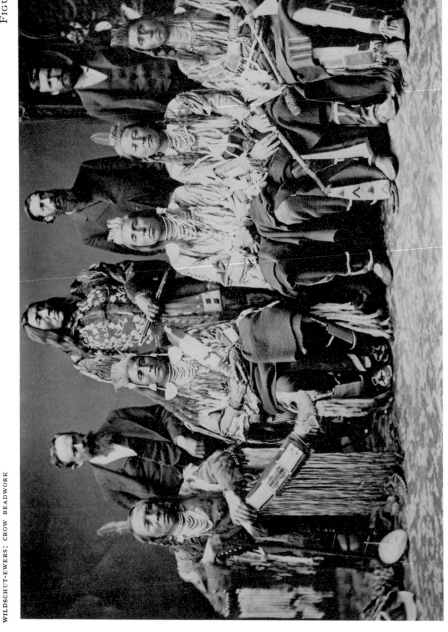

CROW DELEGATION IN WASHINGTON, 1880

FIGURE 3

MAIHF CAT. NO. 12/3099. SPREAD OF SLEEVES. 47 IN.

FIGURE 4

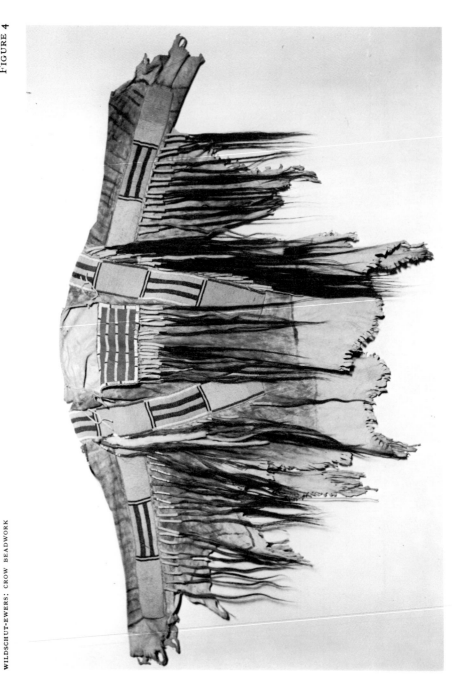

A CROW BEADED SHIRT

MAIHF CAT. NO. 3/2909. SPREAD OF SLEEVES 58 IN.

FIGURE 5

DETAIL OF A CROW BEADED SHIRT

MAIHF CAT. NO. 22/1697 LENGTH OF BEADED SLEEVE-STRIP, 15 IN.

FIGURE 6

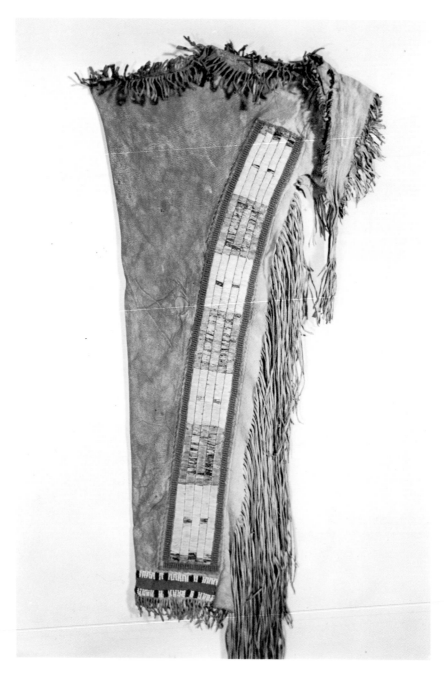

QUILLED AND BEADED LEGGING   MAIHF CAT. NO. 1/6931. LENGTH, 32 IN.

CROW INDIANS AT FORT UNION, 1851.   COURTESY OF THE SMITHSONIAN INSTITUTION
AFTER A PENCIL DRAWING BY R. F. KURZ.

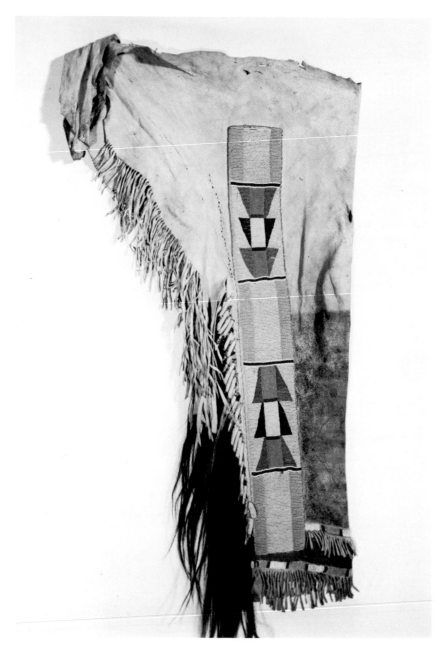

BEADED LEGGING   MAIHF CAT. NO. 1/1067. LENGTH, 36 IN.

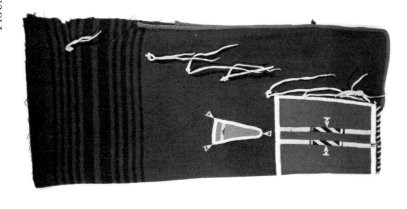

10. BEADED BLANKET — CLOTH LEGGING
MAIHF CAT. NO. 11/7687. LENGTH, 30^1/$_2$ IN.

9. CROW WARRIOR WEARING BLANKET
CLOTH LEGGINGS.
FROM CARL WIMAR'S SKETCHBOOK,
1858.
COURTESY CITY ART MUSEUM, ST. LOUIS

HOLDS-HIS-ENEMY
PHOTOGRAPHED IN WASHINGTON, 1910
COURTESY OF THE SMITHSONIAN INSTITUTION

CHIEF PLENTY COUPS
PHOTOGRAPHED IN WASHINGTON, 1913

COURTESY OF THE SMITHSONIAN INSTITUTION

14. WOMAN'S DRESS DECORATED WITH
IMITATION ELK TEETH AND BEADWORK

MAIHF CAT. NO. 12/6406,
LENGTH 47 IN.

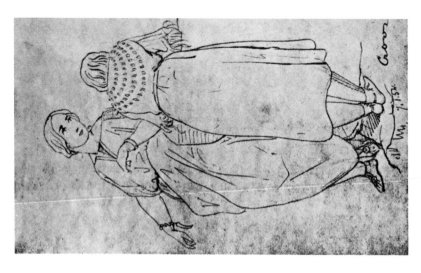

13. CROW INDIAN WOMEN AT FORT UNION,
1852

AFTER PENCIL DRAWING BY R. F. KURZ

COURTESY OF THE SMITHSONIAN INSTITUTION

16. GIRL'S AND WOMAN'S BEADED LEGGINGS.
MAIHF CAT. NOS. 11/5334; 11/7691. LENGTH, 20½ IN.

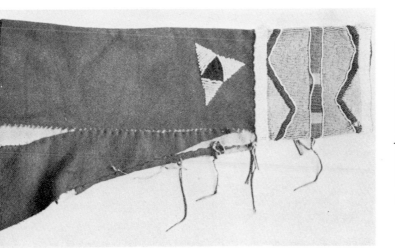

15. WOMAN'S BEADED LEGGING
USNM CAT. NO. 154,357
COURTESY OF THE SMITHSONIAN INSTITUTION

WILDSCHUT-EWERS: CROW BEADWORK

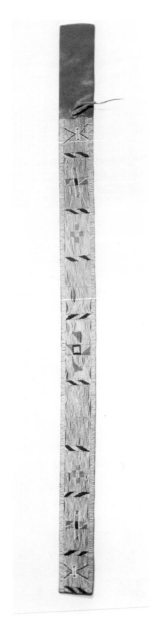

MAIHF CAT. NO. 18/4758. LENGTH, 44½ IN.

17. BEADED BELT

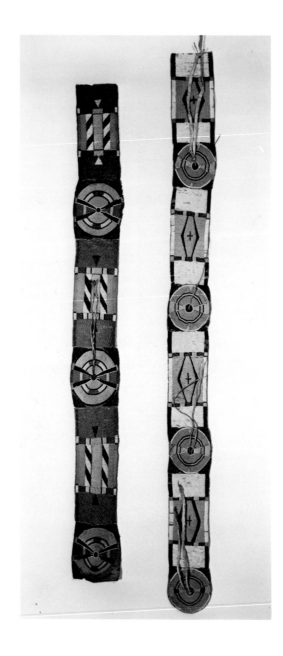

MAIHF CAT. NOS. (TOP) 16/7244; 5/8152, LENGTH 66 IN.

18. BEADED BLANKET STRIPS

FIGURE 19

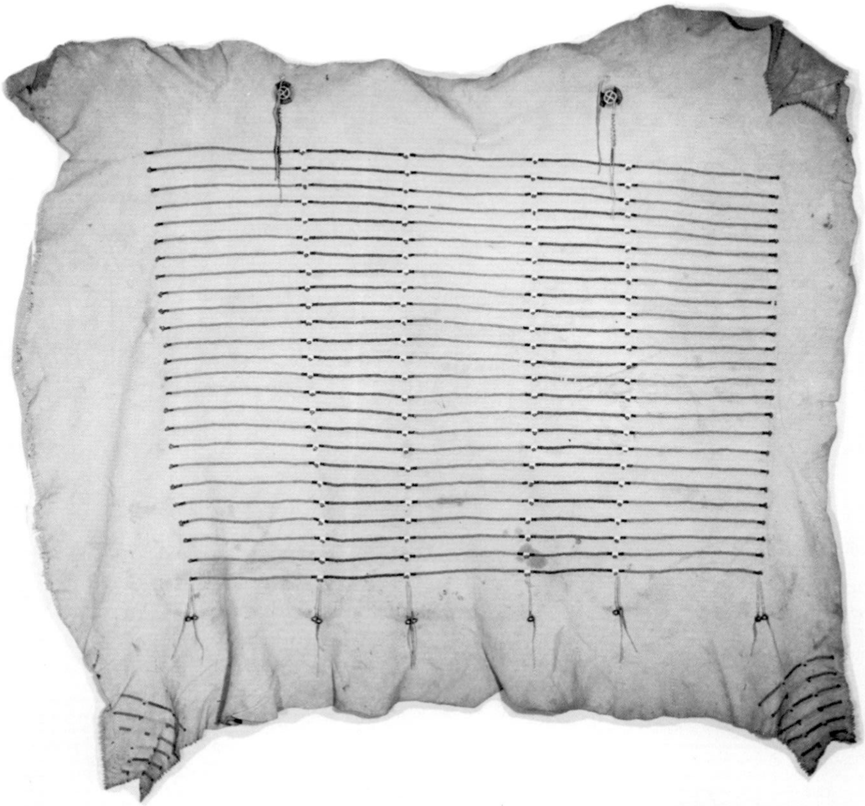

BEADED ELK SKIN ROBE

MAIHF CAT. NO. 13/2263. SIZE, 70 × 54 IN.

20. BUFFALO-HIDE WINTER MOCCASINS OF OLD SOFT-SOLED TYPE.
MAIHF CAT. NO. 14/2122. LENGTH, 10 IN.

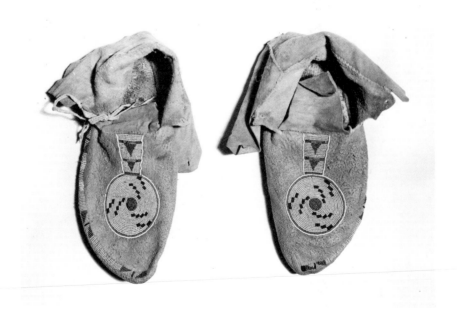

21. HARD-SOLED MOCCASINS BEARING OLD "ROUND BEADWORK" DESIGN.
MAIHF CAT. NO. 3/2925. LENGTH, 11 1/2 IN.

FIGURE 22

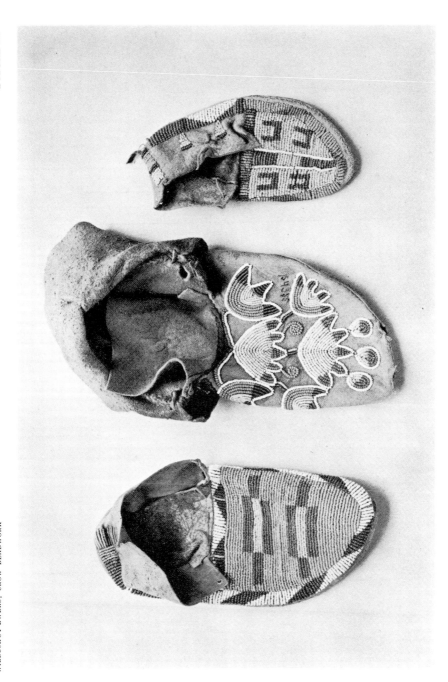

BEADED HARD-SOLED MOCCASINS. COLLECTED BY W. J. HOFFMAN IN 1892.
USNM CAT. NOS. (L-R) 154,354, 154,355, 154,356

FIGURE 23

BEADED HARD-SOLED MOCCASINS BEARING
TYPICAL CROW GEOMETRIC DESIGNS

MAIHF CAT. NOS. (L) 11/8006, LENGTH 9½ IN.; 11/8008

MAIHF CAT. NOS. (L-R) 11/7699; 11/8007; 11/8000; 11/8002, LENGTH, 10$^1/_2$ IN.

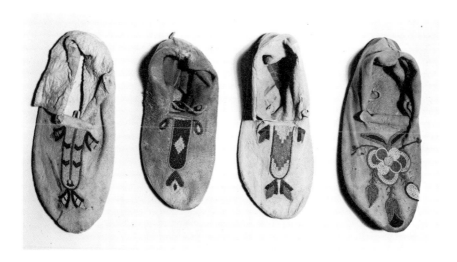

BEADED HARD-SOLED MOCCASINS.
MAIHF CAT. NOS. (L-R) 11/8003; 11/8004; 11/8005; 11/8001, LENGTH 10$^1/_2$ IN.

FIGURE 25

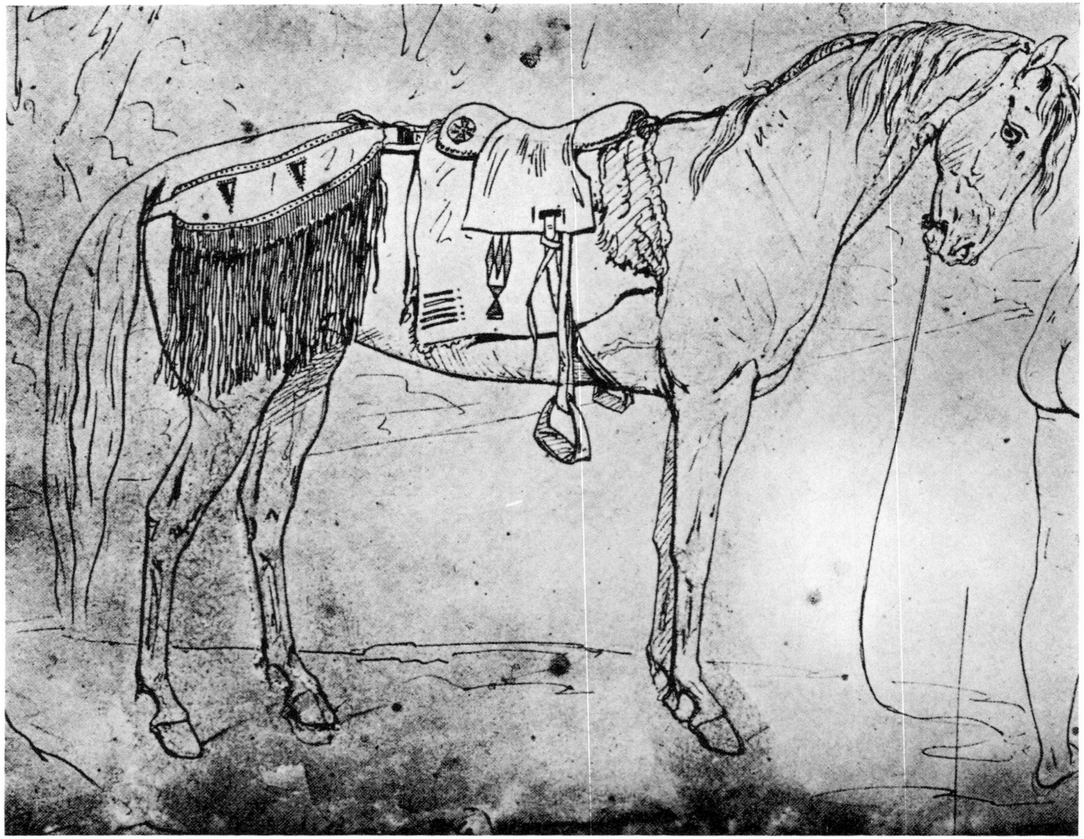

A SADDLED CROW INDIAN HORSE

AFTER A PENCIL DRAWING BY R. F. KURZ

COURTESY OF THE SMITHSONIAN INSTITUTION

FIGURE 26

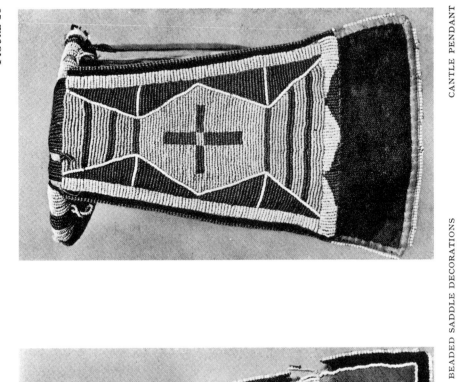

CANTLE PENDANT

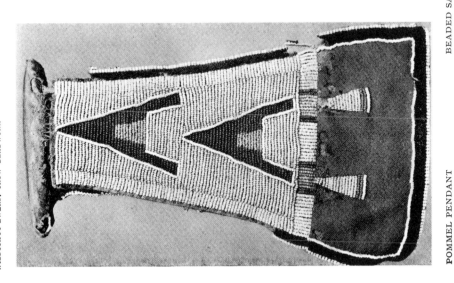

POMMEL PENDANT

BEADED SADDLE DECORATIONS
USNM CAT. NO. 154,368
COURTESY OF THE SMITHSONIAN INSTITUTION

28. BEADED FOREHEAD ORNAMENT
FOR A HORSE

MAIHF CAT. NO. 2/4433. HEIGHT, 12 IN.

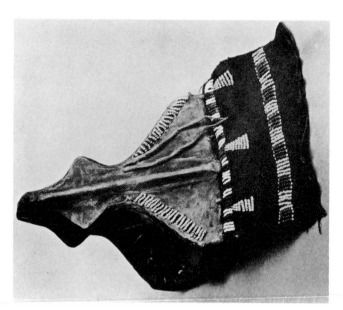

27. BEADED STIRRUP ATTACHED TO WOMAN'S SADDLE.
COLLECTED PRIOR TO 1868. USNM CAT. NO. 6,468

COURTESY OF THE SMITHSONIAN INSTITUTION

BEADED CRUPPER FOR A MAN'S HORSE   MAIHF CAT. NO. 12/314. LENGTH 63 IN

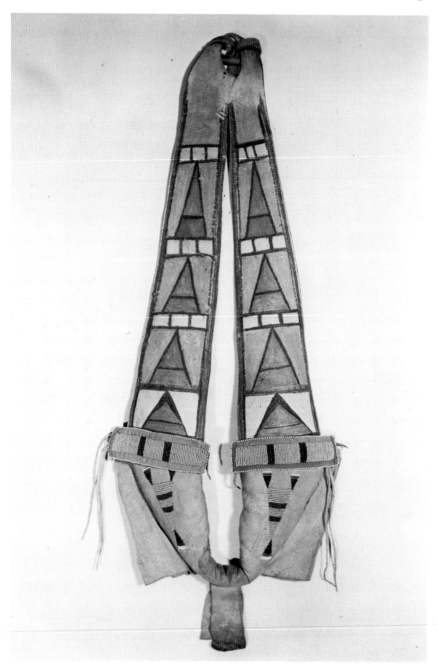

BEADED CRUPPER FOR A WOMAN'S HORSE. MAIHF CAT. NO. 18/9233 A. LENGTH, 33 IN.

FIGURE 31

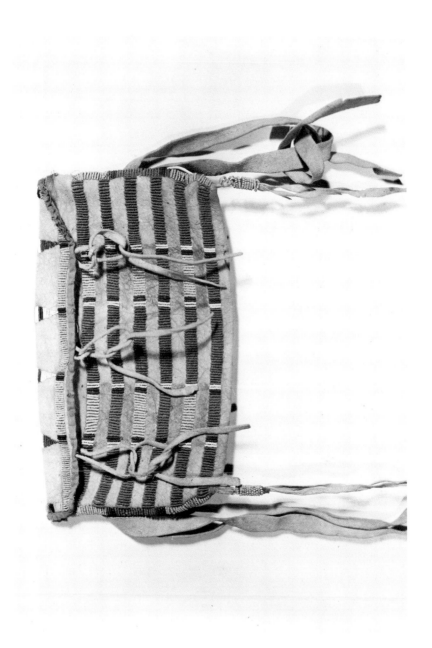

MAIHF CAT. NO. 18/4619. WIDTH, 13³/₄ IN.

BEADED SADDLE BAG

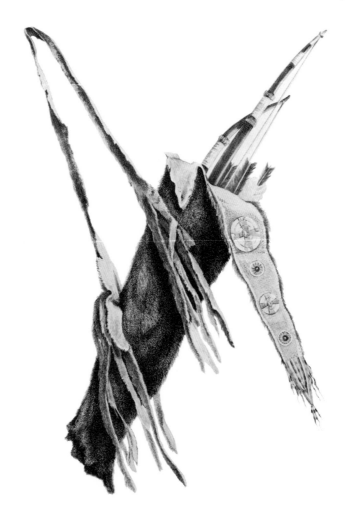

CROW QUILLED AND BEADED QUIVER, 1833.
FROM A LITHOGRAPH AFTER CARL BODMER

COURTESY OF THE SMITHSONIAN INSTITUTION

33. BEADED OTTER SKIN QUIVER. USNM CAT. NO. 164,826

COURTESY OF THE SMITHSONIAN INSTITUTION

34. BEADED GUN CASE. USNM CAT. NO. L 75. LENGTH, 44 IN.

FIGURE 35

BEADED SWORD SCABBARD AND
LANCE CASE

MAIHF CAT. NOS. 8480; 20/7709,
LENGTH 57 IN.

FIGURE 36

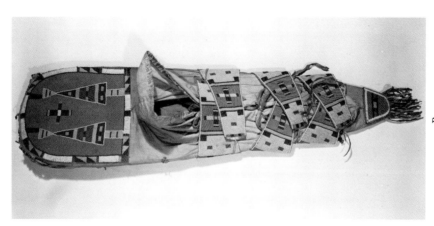

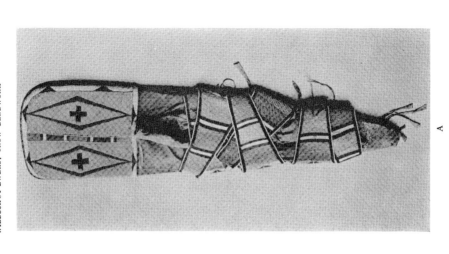

CROW BEADED CRADLES

A: USNM CAT. NO. 154,361 COURTESY OF THE SMITHSONIAN INSTITUTION.   B: MAIHF CAT. NO. 14/821, LENGTH, 42 IN.
C: MAIHF CAT. NO. 2/3140, LENGTH, 42 IN.

A   B   C

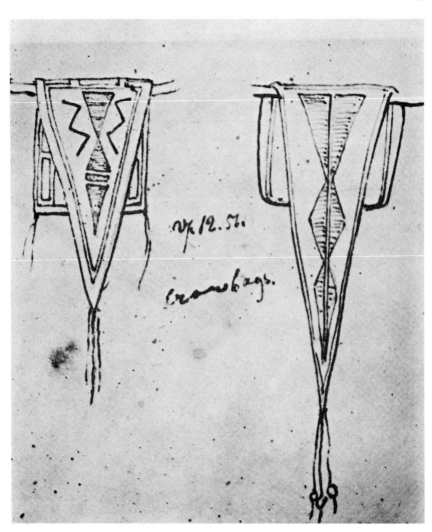

BEADED BELT POUCHES, 1852

AFTER A PENCIL DRAWING BY R. F. KURZ

FIGURE 38

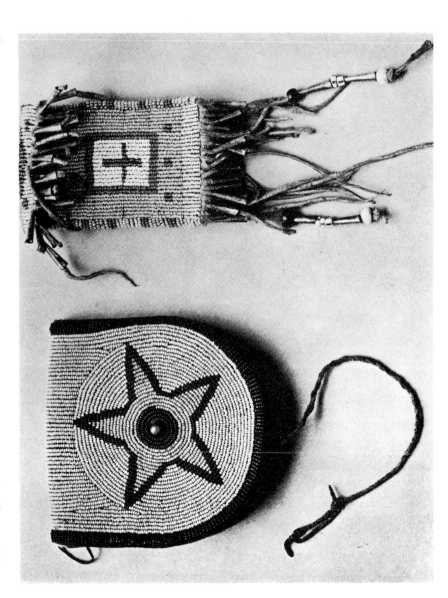

BEADED BELT POUCH AND RATION TICKET POUCH
USNM CAT. NOS. 154,344 (HEIGHT, 5 IN.); 154,345

FIGURES 39, 40

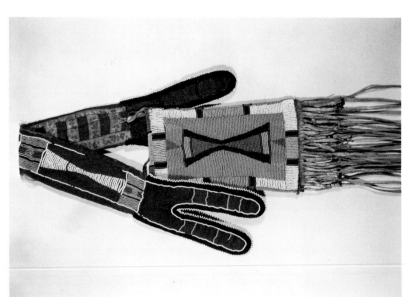

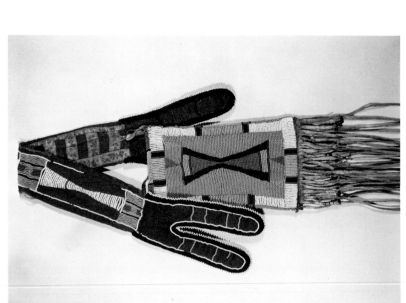

39. BEADED MIRROR POUCH. MAIHF CAT. NO. 20/2871
WIDTH OF POUCH, 5 IN.

40. BEADED PIPE AND TOBACCO POUCH (FRONT AND REAR)
MAIHF CAT. NO. 2/9637. HEIGHT, 28 IN.

FIGURE 41

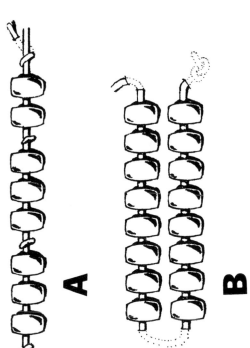

CROW BEADWORK TECHNIQUES

A. OVERLAID OR SPOT STITCH.

B. LAZY STITCH

C. MODIFIED LAZY STITCH, OR CROW STITCH

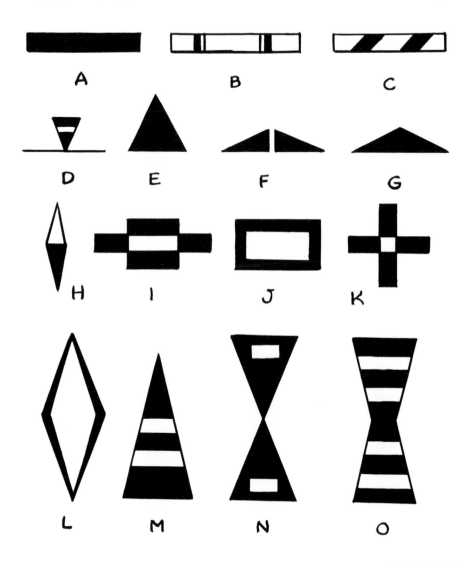

DESIGN ELEMENTS IN CROW BEADWORK

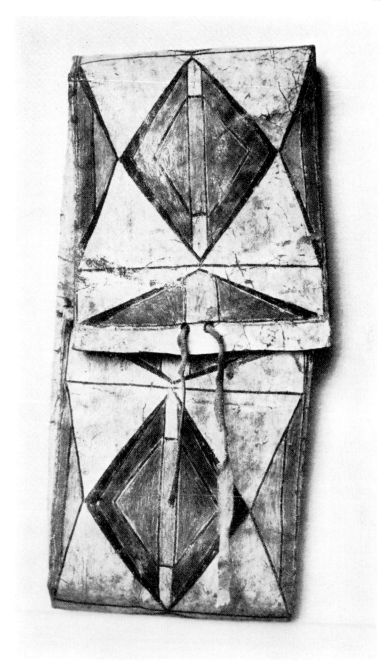

CROW PAINTED PARFLECHE,
COLLECTED PRIOR TO 1889
USNM CAT. NO. 130,574

PAINTED CASE FOR HEADDRESS
MAIHF CAT. NO. 20/7699. LENGTH (CASE ONLY) 21 IN.